MEDIEVAL
GEORGIAN ENAMELS
OF RUSSIA

MEDIEVAL GEORGIAN ENAMELS OF RUSSIA

TEXT BY

SHALVA AMIRANASHVILI

Director of the Georgian National Museum of Fine Arts, Tiflis

HARRY N. ABRAMS, INC., PUBLISHERS, NEW YORK

Translated by François Hirsch and John Ross

Library of Congress Catalog Card Number: 64-11576
Colorplates printed in France. Text printed in Holland. Bound in Holland

LIST OF PLATES

KHAKHULI TRIPTYCH *(continued)*

MEDIEVAL
GEORGIAN ENAMELS
OF RUSSIA

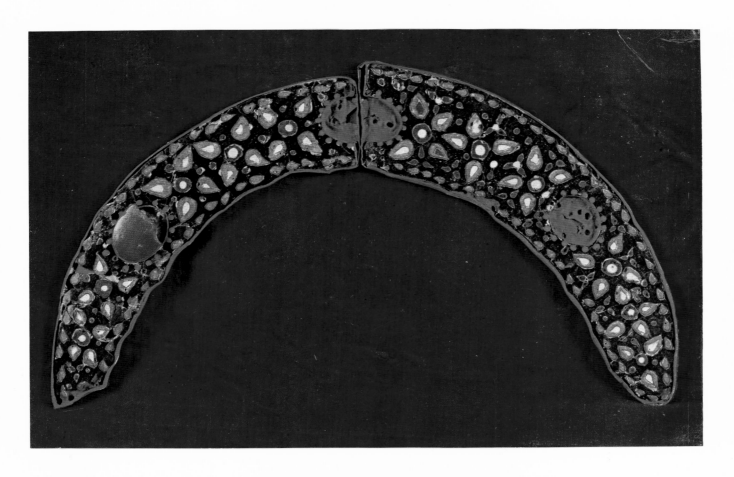

FRAGMENT OF A HALO. 10TH CENTURY

THE ART OF ENAMELING ON GOLD

THE ART OF ENAMELING ON GOLD is considered, with good reason, to be the highest point reached by the decorative arts in ancient Georgia. By virtue of their number and artistic qualities, and the special interest they present for scholars, Georgian enamels constitute one of the most important bodies of artwork in the entire world.

The enameled gold objects that have survived take the form of icons, medallions intended to adorn icon frames, manuscript bindings, crosses, panagias, reliquaries, and so on. The first scientific classification of Georgian enamels was made by N. P. Kondakov, who was also the first to draw the dividing line between Byzantine and Georgian work, the latter being recognizable by its brilliant coloring and the techniques used in execution. In short, he revealed to the world the finest pieces inherited from the days of enamelwork in Georgia.

N. P. Kondakov made a detailed study of enamels, not only in private collections, but also *in situ*, in the course of a journey undertaken with A. Bakradze, the great specialist in Georgian history and art. Unfortunately, in spite of the capital contribution Kondakov made to the study of enamels, he estimated the artistic value of Georgian enamelwork exclusively in terms of its resemblance to Byzantine models. In his opinion Georgian and Slavonian enamels were only adulterated, provincial variants of Byzantine art; the real significance of Georgian and ancient Russian enamels escaped the great specialist.

Kondakov maintained that the refined techniques in use among the artists of Byzantium were beyond the reach of the Georgians, and that only those enamels distinguished by primitive technique and bright colors could be attributed to them. However, if this *a priori* conception is subjected to critical analysis, one comes to rather different conclusions.

Georgian enamelwork embraces several currents and tendencies. The existence of a whole series of dated works has made it possible to establish an accurate picture of the art's historical evolution, which must be taken into account in order to classify and analyze the works in question.

In the last few years important discoveries have been made in the study of Georgian cloisonné enamels, particularly where techniques are concerned. Experimental research has revealed how Georgian and Byzantine smalts were prepared, and has made it possible to execute copies of tenth- and eleventh-century Georgian cloisonné enamels. Byzantine and Georgian enamels differ in the chemical composition of the materials used—the different smalts—which seems to indicate that Georgian artists made considerable use of local materials. Indeed, it is certain that the "wine-dark glow" of the Georgian smalts used to convey flesh tones—which, as Kondakov shrewdly pointed out, constitutes the basic line of separation between Byzantine and Georgian enamels—is closely linked to the presence of manganese.

The enamels vary in the composition of the vitreous mass and in the way the supporting metal plate is prepared. Differences in the composition of the enamel itself depend on several factors: chemical composition, the skill of the glass-blower, and the artistic tendency of the school in question. Generally, Georgian and Byzantine enamels were executed on very fine gold. The vitreous mass can be prepared in many ways, but all are variants on the basic procedures used in the manufacture of lead or potassium glass, with the addition of metallic oxides to obtain the desired color. The lead serves to increase the fusibility of the vitreous mass.

Enamels can be divided into three classes, depending on the way the smalt is applied to the metal: champlevé (hollowed-out), cloisonné (partitioned), and painted work.

Cloisonné enameling, which requires considerable technical skill and a highly developed artistic sense, is the most widely used in Georgian art.

Only one specimen of champlevé work is known: an icon on gold—formerly conserved in the town of Jumati, but now lost—representing the Archangels Michael and Gabriel. Kondakov dated this work in the thirteenth or fourteenth century and, basing his argument on style, coloring, and execution, considers it a Georgian work: "The outlines of the heads, wings, and garments are worked in relief in the gold panel, using the technique proper to champlevé work, instead of cloisonné, which is always the case in Byzantine art."

The process used in the preparation of the smalt is now quite well known. The glass was crushed and then ground to a fine powder in special mortars. This powder was kept in separate containers, one container for each color. After this operation a metal panel was prepared—gold in the cases that will concern us—and the enamel was applied.

In champlevé work the cavities intended for the colors of the motif are chiseled into the surface of the plate itself, leaving the outlines intact and in relief. Generally, the inside of these cavities is rough, thus allowing the smalt to adhere more firmly to the metal. Each is filled with powder of the appropriate color that has been moistened into a paste. The piece of work is then left to dry in the air and when all moisture is eliminated, it is fired in an oven. When fusion is complete the plate is removed from the oven, with great care; precautions are taken to ensure slow, constant cooling, for if cooled too rapidly the enamel is liable to split and break away from the metal surface. When the work is sufficiently cool, more of the appropriate smalt paste is spread in the various compartments and the piece is fired again. This operation is repeated until the surface of the enamel, after cooling, is level with the metal outlines. Finally, the surface of the enameled plate is evened off with wet sandstone and polished until it is smooth and shiny.

In Georgia, as in Byzantium, enamelwork called for the most complex and refined techniques. In fact, the greater part of Byzantine enamels were made on gold, using the cloisonné method.

When one makes a close study of cloisonné enamels in general, giving particular attention to damaged specimens, it is possible to determine almost all the important stages of their manufacture, as well as many technical details. If the entire surface of the plate is to be covered with enamel, one can either turn up the edges of the plate or solder on a low border, also in gold. If, on the other hand, only a given part of the plate is to be enameled, the expanse covered by the entire motif is chiseled out with a gouge to the desired depth. This explains why a gouge was discovered in the course of the excavations carried out by V. Khvoïko near the Desyatinnaya (Cathedral of the Dormition of the Virgin) in Kiev. Normally, the supporting material is covered with a thin plate of gold which is hollowed

MEDALLION OF AN ARCHANGEL.
12TH CENTURY

out according to the motifs chosen, great care being taken to avoid tearing it. Next, the artist traces the outlines of the subject on the plate with a fine needle, bends tiny bands of gold into shape with pliers, and then, using pincers, places and fixes the bands onto the plate. The bands follow the lines of the composition exactly, serving as partitions and forming a completely closed compartment for each color. The ground of the plate, inside the partitions, is then grooved and roughened to ensure better adhesion of the enamel mass. When one remembers that cloisonné enamels were made on a very small scale, so that the diameter of a face was often only about an eighth of an inch, one can only marvel at the minute accuracy of the artist's work.

But the principal difficulty presented by the manufacture of cloisonné enamel is precisely the soldering of the partitions, since the work is far too delicate for fire to be used. In this connection, the declarations of specialists who maintain that the solder used was wax or cherry glue (B. Rybakov) appear inexact. It is certain that in ancient times a process of solid soldering without fire was known and used exclusively for the execution of art objects in gold. This process gave rise to the technique employed in the granulated and filigree decoration of goldsmith's work. "Granulated work," in particular, a technique that entails fixing minute grains of gold on a plate of the same metal, requires exceptional manual skill and fine execution.

The tiny gold globules are prepared in advance from very small fragments of metal, then placed on the surface to be decorated. As for the method used in ancient times, it is difficult to imagine exactly what it could have been. Presumably the molten metal was poured through a sieve into a vessel containing cold water, thus separating the metal into fine drops. The cold granules of metal were then sorted according to size, for this procedure did not produce identically sized drops. It is perfectly possible that the shot thus obtained was then shaken in a closed container to give it a smooth, shiny surface. In his famous treatise on the goldsmith's art, Benvenuto Cellini tells us that the metal was covered with a weak glue extracted from pear seeds, onto which the granules were carefully placed. After drying, these gold granules were dusted with a soldering preparation, in some cases composed of borax, then the plate was fired.

The granulated technique used in the goldsmith's work discovered in Georgia can be traced back to about fifteen hundred years before our time.

One of the masterpieces of this period is the magnificent silver-gilt cup with filigree and granulated decoration, set with stones, turquoises, and pale pink coraline, that was discovered in a tumulus at T'rialet'i dating from about 1500 B.C. The decoration of the outside of the cup was executed separately: it was a sheet of gold, engraved in a spiral leaf pattern, onto which the elements of the design were soldered. The sheet was firmly fitted over the entire surface of the cup and fixed around the edge with hooks hidden by artful soldering.

The polychrome decoration relates this cup to other objects found in the same tumulus, in particular a bead found in tumulus 17. Originally part of a gold necklace, it was adorned with colored stones and granulated work. This piece recalls the Neo-Mycenaean stone discovered at Vaphio, dating from after 1500 B.C.

The technique of granulated decoration is also found in Troy at the level of the second city. However, the most ancient examples of this ornamental procedure—the use of granulated and filigree techniques—come from the imperial tombs at Ur (about 3000 B.C.). B. Kuftin has rightly pointed out that large spherical beads are not found in Sumer, where filigree was more widely used than granulated work.

The archaeological material we possess at present does not enable us to follow the later development of Georgian jewelry, remarkable as it was, as it was revealed in the Middle Bronze Age monuments of T'rialet'i. Until the Achaemenid period (from 688 to 330 B.C.) gold and silver disappeared from funerary objects and treasures. We have to wait until the beginning of the fifth century B.C. for the reappearance in Georgia of precious dishes and ornaments, the remains of a highly refined art. The most significant work from this period is the Akhalgori Treasure, which is closely linked to Georgian tradition. This monument dates from immediately after the objects discovered at Kazbek, including works from the villages of Partshanakanevi and Nossiri.

We still do not know of any works that bridge the gap between this jewelry production and that stimulated by the presence of deposits of precious metals in Georgia during the Middle Bronze Age. However, the study of the techniques used in jewelry during this period proves that social and cultural conditions, fostering the development of a prosperous, refined jewelry art, survived in Georgia from very early in its ancient history right up to the first centuries of our era.

The T'rialet'i gold beads, which date from the Middle Bronze Age, are adorned with bezels intended for set stones, and granulated decoration which forms a pleasant linear ornament firmly applied to the surface of the bead. Furthermore, the surfaces of the largest spherical elements of the necklace are dotted with little gold cabochons. These are shaped like pinheads and are fixed to the outside of the piece; the end of each pin was probably split inward, then clinched with a hammer. The barely visible cabochons on the other pieces were probably beaten in repoussé, the granules being cold-soldered to the surface of the work.

All these technical procedures used in decorating goldsmith's work are to be found almost without modification in the Akhalgori Treasure. The first thing that strikes one when examining the gold objects in this treasure is the generous use of applied granules. However, the granules themselves are finer, the soldering more delicate and accomplished, and

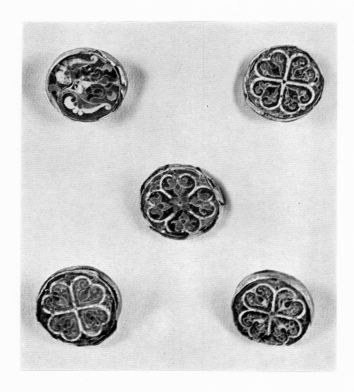

ENAMELED ROSETTES FROM
THE TSALENDGIKA ICON

ENAMELED ROSETTES FROM
THE KHOBI ICON

the pattern more rigorous and sober in style. The decoration of earrings remains faithful to the technique of cabochons fastened beneath the surface of the piece.

The study of goldsmith's work, from the Middle Bronze Age to the first centuries A.D., reveals the high technical qualifications of the ancient Georgian masters, as well as a refined artistic taste that found its own style at each period in its history. The artistic traditions of precious metalwork, and more particularly work in gold, are remarkable for their great stability. The decisive technical factor was the introduction of cold soldering, without which the creation of many pieces and the use of granulated decoration on a large scale would scarcely have been possible.

The objects found in the Akhalgori tombs give a brilliant picture of the level achieved by goldsmith's and jeweler's crafts during the first centuries of the Christian Era. All aspects of jewelry known since earliest antiquity—in particular polychromy, filigree and granulated techniques, gouging and forging—survived until then.

On the other hand, on examination of polychrome decoration, one is faced with new phenomena, typical of the first centuries of the Christian Era, but unknown in ancient times: the polychromy of this period, while still making generous use of precious and semi-precious stones of various colors, also exploits colored glass and cloisonné enamels. Study of the objects found in the lavish tombs of Armaziskheri shows that from the second century A.D. cloisonné enamel plays an important part in polychrome jewelry: a fine example is a gold belt, composed of rectangular plates, in which cloisonné cells are filled with a semi-translucent, monochrome, grayish-white glass. In general, the gold objects from Armaziskheri—all the rings, most of the earrings and bracelets—are adorned with polished set stones of various colors and shapes, and sometimes with glass and enamel.

Thus in the first centuries of our era Georgia boasted a school of jewelry and gold-smith's work that continued an original, centuries-old tradition, its ancient origins linking it to the industry of the Middle Bronze Age. It is possible to retrace the development of taste and style over this long period of Georgian culture, for the fundamental conquests of technique in this field survive for many centuries. But at the same time, with the appearance and introduction into daily life of a new material, glass, and especially after the discovery of a process for making colored glass, an important transformation takes place in the polychromy of jewelry. The first cloisonné enamels appear in the second century A.D.

The most difficult operation in making these enamels is the soldering of the gold partitions, for as the use of fire is absolutely ruled out, soldering must be done cold. I. Taruash-vili, a research chemist attached to the Georgian National Museum of Fine Arts, has made an experimental study of this technique. His experiments have thrown light on several points. Firstly, they showed that Georgian enamelers had been using cold soldering since the Middle Bronze Age, and secondly, that the solder used consisted of a gold-based alloy. Taruashvili then advanced the hypothesis that the master jewelers of Antiquity used mercury which, as we know, has the property of dissolving gold. In order to fix the partitions to the surface of the work, the plate was covered with mercury; the thin fillets of gold were then placed on the surface following the outlines of the motif, and the result was a solid soldering. After carefully checking these observations and hypotheses Taruashvili executed copies of ancient Georgian cloisonné enamels in the National Museum of Fine Arts. He even managed to determine precisely how the various smalts for the essential colors were prepared, and then proceeded with experiments which confirmed his findings. As far as cold soldering is concerned, the procedure used by the ancient masters to decorate their works with applied granules must have been the same as that described above.

The discovery of the method of cold soldering on gold made it possible to reply conclusively to the question of the origin of Georgian cloisonné enamels. Until now the problem has been treated in terms of *a priori* conceptions, without taking archaeological data sufficiently into account. Most scholars who have studied the history of enamelwork judge that the art was born in the East. However, study of art objects in precious metals, in particular gold objects from the early Christian Era, shows that production of enameled objects could not have originated in and spread from a single center. Byzantine champlevé and cloisonné enamels, Georgian and ancient Russian enamelwork are the original products of ancient local traditions of the goldsmith's and jeweler's arts.

In the history of jewelry, cloisonné gold objects set with glass functioned as replacement articles; to economize on precious stones, glass imitations were used. The technique of cold soldering and the perfection of methods for making colored glass provided the technical basis that ensured the development of Byzantine, Georgian, and Russian enamelwork. Moreover, at the same time the Christian ideal had endowed the ancient art of enameling with a new content in accordance with the period's religious aspirations. Cloisonné enamels treating Christian themes appear at the same time in Byzantium and Georgia, at the end of the sixth century. N. P. Kondakov considered that the art of cloisonné enameling in Russia depended on Byzantine influence after the conversion of Russia to Christianity during the reign of Yaroslav the Good. But taking the monk Theophilus' treatise as his basis, B. Rybakov places the emergence of a Russian school of cloisonné enamel in the second half of the tenth century, at the time of Olga and Sviatoslav. Indeed this treatise, which the most recent works by specialists date in the second half of the tenth century rather than, as was formerly believed, the eleventh or twelfth, mentions *"carefully worked"* Russian enamels. A center of champlevé enamelwork existed in the central Dniepr region in the fourth and fifth centuries of our era. Toward the middle of the tenth century the craftsmen of Kiev, after contact with Byzantium, abandoned champlevé technique for cloisonné; in the eleventh century they were preparing the enamel themselves and their hands were becoming more skillful.

Existing Georgian cloisonné enamels on religious subjects—which we shall analyze later—indicate that they made their appearance in Georgia in the seventh century at the latest. During the reign of Constantine Porphyrogenitus (A.D. 913–959) enamels were widely used in religious and daily life, for instance the holy vases—ciboria, patens, and chalices—reliquaries, and icon frames, which are referred to by a general name of Greek origin.

From the eleventh century on, as we can see from documents of Georgian origin, the word signifying enamel derived from the old Russian term *Khiminet*, which later became *finift*. However, in ancient Georgia another word was used for enamel, *minai*, which was very widely used from the sixth century on. In Arabic this word is used for enamel, mosaic, or glaze, and we find it in Persian with the same sense. In the latter language the composite word *minakar* is used for the enameled work. The same term is to be found later in Georgia,

MEDALLIONS OF SAINTS PAUL (*above*),
DEMETRIUS (*below left*), AND PETER (*below right*)
FROM THE TSALENDGIKA ICON

but not before the seventeenth century, and consequently, in a period when the technique of cloisonné enameling had long fallen into disuse.

The records relative to the donation made by the Catholicos, Melchisedek, to the Svetiskhoveli Cathedral in Mtskhet'i in A.D. 1029, indicate that the Catholicos was giving the chapter a gold chalice and paten, decorated with stones, beads, and enameled icons.

In the Georgian text recording the foundation of the Petritsion monastery the two terms *minai* and *shemephton* are used with the same meaning. The fact that these two expressions figure in the Georgian text indicates that the word *minai* referred to the smalt, and *shemephton* to cloisonné enamel.

N. P. Kondakov considers the Arabic word *minai* Indo-European in origin. In his opinion it is not a Semitic word. Besides, Kremer points out that in the second century after the Hegira the Arabs were manufacturing colored glass. In the Avesta (sacred books of the ancient Zoroastrian religion), *mina* means precious necklace. It is certain that this word is at the root of the Pahlavi (Persian) *mineak*, the Greek *maniakis*, and the Armenian *maneak*.

From Georgian chronicles, historical documents, and records of donations it appears that Byzantine, as well as native works, were highly appreciated in Georgia. In this connection it is worth stressing the particular space reserved in chronicles and other documents

MEDALLIONS OF SAINTS GEORGE (*above left*),
JOHN (*above right*), AND LUKE (*below right*), AND THE
VIRGIN (*below left*) FROM THE TSALENDGIKA ICON

for works coming from other countries, especially Byzantium. The *Matiané Kartilisai'*
chronicle reports that Melchisedek, the Catholicos of Georgia already mentioned, went to
Constantinople twice, the first time during the reign of the Emperor Basil (A.D. 976–1025)
and later, during the reign of Romanus (A.D. 1028–1034). In a record of the donation made
to the Svetiskhoveli Cathedral, Catholicos Melchisedek indicates that the Emperor Constantine gave a gold icon representing the Saviour; the Emperor Basil, an icon of the
Mother of God adorned with gold, precious stones, and pearls; the Emperor Romanus,
sacerdotal vestments woven with gold, and so on. The text also stresses the gifts made by
Bagrat IV.

The record of the donation is extremely precise. It describes down to the last detail the
objects from Byzantium—a large basin and a jug—as well as a basin and jug of Greek
workmanship.

This precision shows the particular attention paid to all things Byzantine. On the other
hand, no mention was made of precious religious or secular objects when they were local
work. Georgian chronicles speak of fabulous treasures and marvelous objects that were
at one time common. In the history of the Queen Tamara we read: "All the State treasuries
filled up with gold and golden utensils, for the gold flowed like sand, precious stones and
pearls were counted in whole measures." The lengths of cloth of gold from Greece and

other lands were cast aside as useless baubles, for all their immense cost. The imperial court scorned silver vessels; everything was made of gold and crystal, set with rare ornaments and precious stones from the Indies, which the Queen distributed generously to the churches for the celebration of the Mass. To paraphrase one of Queen Tamara's historians, Georgia had become so rich that "peasants lived like gentlemen, gentlemen like princes and princes like Kings."

Other documents attest to the extraordinary wealth of the Georgian sacristies, monasteries, and churches, which survived the Mongol invasions, at the time when the country was also struggling to maintain its independence against Turkey and Iran. European travelers and, in particular, Catholic missionaries speak eloquently of these treasures (Tavernier, M. Chardin, Lamberti, Castelli).

However, the most detailed documents that we possess on Georgian repoussé and enamel work are to be found in the reports drawn up by Russian diplomatic missions, and written by men highly competent in matters of Christian art and iconography—as we can see from the account drawn up by Squire Toloshanov and Deacon Ievlev after their embassy to Imeret'i (1650–1652), the mission to Dadiani carried out by Deacon Elchin and the priest Pavel Zakharev, and so on. Furthermore, whereas the fabulous riches of Georgia had once merely excited the envy of foreign invaders, during the second half of the nineteenth century many collectors were actually successful in laying their hands on precious specimens of Georgian repoussé and enamel work, which were then scattered in various countries. Fortunately, today all this material is catalogued and has been extensively treated in publications.

The celebrated Khakhuli icon, with its image of the Virgin and its frame decorated with Georgian and Byzantine enamels, was the first to attract the attention of collectors. The pillage of the monastery of Gelati was systematically organized in 1856. The objective was to gain possession of the enameled *Deisis* icon of the Virgin in Prayer, a Georgian work dating from the second half of the tenth century, placed in a large engraved coffer in the form of a triptych.

This icon entered the collection of Botkin, who mentions it in a monograph devoted to the enamels of the Zvenigorodskoi, Schulz, and Botkin collections. This image of the Virgin was restored to Georgia in 1923 and is now in the National Museum of Fine Arts. Moreover, many enameled icons were removed from the metal frame of the Khakhuli Virgin and replaced with painted enamels, modern Russian work in which care was taken to reproduce the original Georgian inscriptions.

Similarly, panels of gold set with enamels, which had formed part of a Georgian gospel binding, disappeared from the monastery of Gelati. The original plates were replaced with a silver panel, the work of Sazik, and the enamels became part of the Balashov collection

(Kondakov reproduces them on the end-papers of his monograph). The panels from this gospel have been dispersed; one, representing Saint Demetrius, is now in the Schlossmuseum, Berlin, and the other is in Belgium, in the Stvelet collection. On the grounds of the alleged need for restoring the ancient icons of Jumati and Shemoshmedi in western Georgia, these monasteries were persuaded to part with two images, one of the Archangel Michael, the other of the Archangel Gabriel. The former was adorned with locally made enamel icons and bore inscriptions in Georgian.

The enamels set in the frame of the Archangel Gabriel icon were also Georgian, but their inscriptions were in Greek. This icon originally held twelve medallions; when it was removed from the monastery of Jumati the enamel of Saint Mark was already missing. The Zvenigorodskoi collection contained nine enamels, representing the Saviour, the Virgin, John the Baptist, Saints Peter, Paul, Matthew, Luke, John, and George; they were published with a note by Kondakov, and are now conserved in the Metropolitan Museum of Art in New York. The image of Saint Demetrius passed from the Botkin collection to the Louvre. Lastly, a medallion carrying the image of Saint Theodore, also from the Botkin collection, is now in the Georgian National Museum of Fine Arts.

The nine enameled medallions that formerly decorated the icon of the Archangel Michael passed into various collections. The enamels of the Saviour and Saint Demetrius figured in the Botkin collection before being listed in the catalogue of the Georgian National Museum of Fine Arts. The medallion of Saint George was part of the Bobrinski collection; the whereabouts of the medallion of Saint Theodore is still unknown. Lastly, the ten medallions representing the Virgin, John the Baptist, the Evangelists Mark and John, and the Apostles Peter and Paul, which were kept in the monastery of Shemoshmedi, were destroyed. Shortly after the October Revolution, some fragments of the repoussé decoration from the icon of the Archangel Michael passed into the Hermitage Museum collection and were published by L. Maculevitch.

A fine image of the Archangels Michael and Gabriel, executed in champlevé enamel, was also removed from the monastery of Jumati and has disappeared without a trace.

The Museo Lázaro Goldiano in Madrid possesses twelve enamel medallions representing the Saviour, Virgin (*Deisis*), the Evangelists Matthew and Mark, the Apostles Phillip, Paul, and Simon, Saints Nicholas, John Chrysostom, and Theodore, the Virgin Enthroned with the Child, the Saviour, and two smaller medallions with an eagle for John the Evangelist and a bull for Saint Luke. These enamels belonged to Botkin, who published them himself. V. Jobadze-Tsitsishvili dates them in the sixth century, and sees traces of Georgian workmanship in some of them.

According to Kondakov, before the Revolution the sacristy of the Palace Chapel of Libadia sheltered a cross intended to hold a fragment of the Tree of Life. This cross,

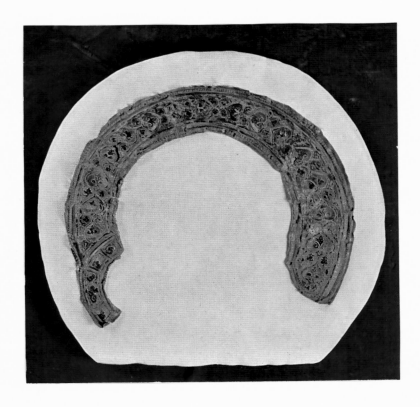

adorned with enamels representing Constantine and Helena, is now in a special reserve of the Pushkin Museum in Moscow.

The gold reliquary carrying an enameled medallion of Saint George belonged to the Empress K'et'evan of Kakhet'i, martyred by Shah Abbas in 1624, and was published by O. Dalton.

The masterpiece of the art of ancient Georgia, decorated with cloisonné enamels of the thirteenth century, is kept in the sacristy of the Church of the Resurrection in Jerusalem. Kondakov provides a photograph and gives a detailed description of this magnificent icon of the Saviour. According to Professor A. Tsagareli this icon was probably restored in 1770. Unfortunately Professor Tsagareli has not completed cleaning the ancient Georgian inscription placed on the metal frame beneath the image of the Saviour. To judge by Kondakov's photograph, this image must have been remade entirely in 1770. Given the form of the enameled halo, Christ must have been shown in bust in the coffin, His head slightly tilted to the right. The presence of half-length weeping angels, executed in cloisonné enamel, confirms this observation. This image of the Saviour is the oldest example of an iconographical type very widespread in Italian art of the twelfth and thirteenth centuries.

The establishment of the Soviet regime put an end to the pillage of Georgian historical and artistic monuments. In 1922 and 1923, all the art treasures taken from Georgia under the Tsars were restored. An attempt was also made to reassemble all works of art.

In 1945, all the historical and artistic pieces that the Menshevik government had sent abroad were brought back to Georgia from Paris. In 1952, the Khakhuli triptych, a work of universal value because of the quality of its repoussé work and the sumptuous variety of its cloisonné enamels, was taken to Tiflis, where it is now kept in a special room in the Georgian National Museum of Fine Arts.

While Georgian cloisonné enamels have attracted the attention of many eminent scholars, research in this field is far from complete; indeed, serious study has only just begun. The present volume aims at giving a complete picture of the cloisonné enamels kept in the Georgian National Museum of Fine Arts, which has one of the richest collections in the world. In this way the author hopes to make those treasures accessible to everyone, to the general public as well as to scholars. Thus, this book is addressed not only to specialists of the history of cloisonné enamels, but to every lover of the art of the Middle Ages.

THE SMALL MARTVILI TRIPTYCH

This little triptych ($4^{13}/_{16} \times 4^{13}/_{16}''$) on the theme of the *Deisis* no doubt dates from the earliest period of Georgian enamelwork. The outer surfaces of the side panels are divided into four parts, formerly containing plaques of cloisonné enamel. The plaited motif is soldered on and seems to indicate that the border of the triptych was originally decorated with strings of pearls. When the triptych is closed the obverse shows a frame of gilt-silver set with stones. The angels on the side panels, shown as orants, in an attitude of prayer, were no doubt executed separately in repoussé.

The triptych as a whole takes the form of a reliquary intended to hold a composition enameled on a gold ground. The central *Deisis* (Christ flanked by the Virgin and John the Baptist) in cloisonné enamel was held in place by a band of gold firmly soldered around the edge. The central figure of Christ is missing, and parts of the enamel surface are deformed.

A close study of the icon shows that the figure of Christ, of which only the halo with its cross has survived, was executed separately before being inserted in the central part of the composition. Christ was standing on a pedestal, His right hand held out toward the Virgin. The two white disks in the background close to His head symbolize the sun and the moon. A little below, the monogram of Christ is outlined in gold fillets in the form it took in the earliest Byzantine enamels. The Baptist and the Virgin hold out their hands to Christ in an attitude of supplication.

Vegetable-scroll motifs executed in fine gold fillets are placed between the figures; on either side, there are wavy plant motifs with white tips.

The thickness of the partitions is not regular, illustrating that the technique had not yet reached the precision and accomplishment that were to be so outstanding at the end of the tenth century.

The entire enameled surface of the icon is pierced with small openings due, no doubt, to irregular cooling of the vitreous mass; they are especially noticeable where the artist used a yellow smalt. The dark green of the background and the cobalt blue used for the Virgin's lower garments

are distinguished by their translucency, contrasting with the matte surfaces of the white, yellow, and dark-brown smalts.

On the reverse of the reliquary an ornamental border frames four scenes executed in a pictorial style with free niello drawing: *The Nativity*, *The Presentation at the Temple*, *The Descent into Limbo*, and *The Holy Sepulchre*.

The principal composition of the Martvili triptych is certainly one of the most ancient versions of the *Deisis*, a composition which explains the dogma of the Intercession of the Virgin and John the Baptist. Christ is shown enthroned, judging sinning mankind; He is flanked by Mary and John, who plead with Him on the behalf of humanity. The idea of placing John the Baptist and the Virgin together is based on the most ancient texts in the liturgy.

In Christian iconography the sun and moon figure together in the composition of *Majestas Domini* (Christ in Majesty) in the Eastern and Western worlds, particularly in Georgia after the seventh century, and in Crucifixion scenes. The presence of the sun and moon in a *Deisis* bears

28

witness to the philosophical and dogmatic relationship between this and the *Majestas Domini* themes.

Thus, the Martvili triptych associates the idea of the Last Judgment and the Intercession of the Virgin and John the Baptist with that of the greatness and glorification of Jesus Christ who came to save mankind. The figures of the triptych are so indissolubly linked on the philosophical and religious planes that the artist certainly conceived them simultaneously.

The angels on the side panels of the triptych are executed with a delicacy that shows the vitality of the traditions of primitive Christian art. They were cast, chiseled on the obverse, and then gilded. The pictorial relief, the style of the hair, and the suppleness of the forms here find striking analogies in other Georgian works of art, particularly in the relief figures on the Martvili encolpion-pectoral cross.

Because of its general conception and the style and technique of its execution, the Martvili triptych thus turns out to be a thoroughly Georgian work. It can be placed in the eighth or ninth century.

THE MARTVILI PECTORAL CROSS

The Martvili pectoral cross is another specimen of the technique of relief metalwork combined with cloisonné enamel. It is a diptych intended to hold fragments of the Tree of Life.

This cross is solid gold (6″ high, $3^9/_{16}$″ across, and $^3/_4$″ deep). At the top a massive ring adorned with pearls is fixed to a hinge. The entire piece is edged with pearls, emeralds, and turquoises.

The figures were executed separately, cast in pink gold, and then fixed to the surface. The halos and the cross with the figure of Christ were executed beforehand in cloisonné enamel. The appearance of the reliefs on the obverse and reverse of the cross confirms the impression that the process employed was casting rather than repoussé.

On the obverse the figure of Christ, clad in a long, sleeveless tunic, His head slightly tilted to the left, His eyes open, is fixed to the light-blue ground of the cross edged with emerald green. The halo is in sky-blue enamel and bears a small white cross bordered in red. The arms of the pectoral cross bear busts of the Virgin and Saint John turned toward the Saviour, and the Archangels Michael and Gabriel in fullface. The four halos are in blue enamel with red dots, following accepted usage in ancient enamels.

The Greek inscription in red enamel, placed beneath the cross, can be dated on palaeographical grounds in the eighth or ninth century. Certain details of the lettering enable one to conclude that the diptych is the work of a Georgian artist.

On the reverse of the cross the Virgin, in a standing position, carrying the Child on her left arm, is placed on a blue enamel platform. The turquoise-blue halos are marked with red disks and the Child's halo bears a red cross. On either side of the Virgin is a white star-form circled in blue and emerald green. The extremities of the four arms of the cross carry relief fullface busts of the Four Evangelists: Matthew at the top, Mark at the foot, Luke to the left, and John to the right.

The relief figures are of very high artistic quality, with the admirable suppleness of their forms, the delicacy of their drawing, and the harmony of their slightly elongated proportions. The finely drawn folds of the drapery are extremely effective; many examples of this are to be found in early Christian art, which fell heir to the legacies of Greek art.

The elongated proportions and fine hands, as well as the angle of the heads of Mary and Christ, accentuate the spiritual nature of the characters. The same pictorial style appears in the admirably alive, intensely expressive faces. The treatment of hair is equally remarkable for its fine execution. Christ's hair falls on His shoulders, and His beard is rounded. The slightly curved form of the nose is tastefully emphasized. In accordance with tradition, Christ is shown alive, with open eyes. The face of the Mother bending over her Son, the attitude of the Christ Child sitting in Mary's arms, the Four Evangelists, and the half-figures of the Virgin and the Archangels also vouch for the artist's talent. The author shows acute artistic sense in the way he adapts his style to suit the the individuality of each character.

This study of the relief figures of the Martvili pectoral cross suggests that the work probably had many parallels in early Christian art, especially among those works marked by Oriental influences.

VIRGIN AND CHILD. REVERSE OF THE MARTVILI PECTORAL CROSS.
8TH OR 9TH CENTURY

CRUCIFIXION. OBVERSE OF THE MARTVILI PECTORAL CROSS.
8TH OR 9TH CENTURY

THE VARDZIA ICON

The image of the Virgin, known as the Vardzia icon ($21^1/_4 \times 16^3/_{16}''$), is a *Deisis* adorned with an engraved cover dating from the sixteenth century. The Virgin was entirely repainted in oils in the second half of the nineteenth century.

On the reverse an inscription in ancient Georgian alludes to people about whom we know nothing. Howerver, the palaeographical character of the inscription, the style of the repoussé on the obverse and its decoration enable us to date this icon in the second half of the sixteenth century.

THE VIRGIN. VARDZIA ICON. SECOND HALF OF 19TH CENTURY

The icon incorporates several medallions: the Virgin in Prayer, John the Baptist, the Apostles Peter and Paul, and John the Evangelist. Two medallions are missing; the bezels in which they were set are empty.

The style, execution, and coloring of these enamels place them beyond all doubt among the most ancient cloisonné enamels made in Georgia in the eighth and ninth centuries. They are characterized by their fine execution and polish, the depth and translucency of their colors.

The enamel is laid on thickly. The gold partitions render the precise outlines of the motifs, which are freely and pictorially drawn. The semi-translucent emerald green of the background has the beauty of the first cloisonné enamels. The flesh-colored smalt has lilac overtones—this is the famous "wine-dark glow" so characteristic of Georgian enamels. All the Georgian inscriptions

MEDALLIONS OF JOHN THE BAPTIST (*above*),
SAINT PAUL (*center*), AND THE VIRGIN (*below*)
FROM THE VARDZIA ICON. 8TH OR 9TH CENTURY

are in white enamel, and the artist has limited his range of colors to clear, sober tones, avoiding violent contrasts.

Apart from the Virgin and John the Baptist, whose halos are respectively turquoise and dark blue, the heads are ringed with reddish-purple nimbuses. The Virgin and John the Baptist are clothed in purple. The Apostle Peter and John the Evangelist carry crimson books with white pages and light-blue lozenges on the covers.

The style and execution of these enamels indicate that they were all made in the same workshop, probably by the same artist. The manner, coloring, and technique, as well as the palaeographical character of the Georgian inscriptions show more or less precisely the period in which these masterpieces of Georgian cloisonné enamelwork were created—the eighth or ninth century.

THE GOLD CROSS OF SHEMOSHMEDI

The gold cross of Shemoshmedi, an enameled image of the Crucifixion, can be placed in the first half of the tenth century. It formed part of the Botkin collection. Christ is shown on the cross with His eyes closed; the work is the oldest existing specimen of this particular iconographical treatment. The cross is set up on a small, stepped hill symbolizing Golgotha. Below the cross we see the skull of Adam, in accordance with the ancient traditional belief that the Crucifixion took place on the spot where the first man was buried.

The artist has depicted the moment when Christ, whose head has dropped to His shoulder, commits His spirit into the hands of His father. In this conception of the Crucifixion theme, the weeping witnesses stand around the cross with downcast eyes and do not look at Christ.

Behind the Apostle John, we see a woman who has been claimed as Mary Cleophas, the mother of Jacob and Ossia, who was present at the Passion with Mary Magdalene and the Virgin. However, the text of the Gospels simply mentions the presence of Mary, the wife of Cleophas, near the cross, without specifying that she is "the weeping woman turned away from the cross, for all seemed consumed." The strange position of this character, who stands with her back to Saint John, makes us think rather that this Crucifixion is the prototype of an iconographical conception very widespread in the East: Christ is crucified between the Church Triumphant and the Synagogue marked with the brand of infamy. This being so, the person whose back is turned to Saint John can only be the allegorical figure of the Synagogue.

To the right of Christ, another woman catches in a goblet the blood that flows from His pierced side. She, no doubt, personifies the Church of the New Testament.

The figures are regularly drawn, without dryness or sentimentality. The deep, pure tones of the smalt are proof of the high quality of execution. An inscription in ancient Georgian along the arms of the cross reads as follows: *Jesus, glorify the emperor of the Abkhaz.* This is an allusion to the Abkhaz emperor George, who died in 957.

CRUCIFIXION. GOLD CROSS OF SHEMOSHMEDI. FIRST HALF OF 10TH CENTURY

THE MARTVILI PECTORAL CROSS

Another encolpion-cross from Martvili dates from the first half of the tenth century. It is executed in solid red gold and measures $4\frac{1}{4} \times 3\frac{3}{8} \times \frac{3}{4}''$. In appearance it resembles an ancient baptismal cross; between the four branches and at their extremities there are circular ornaments with precious stones set in a ground of blue or green enamel with gold or red-and-gold disks. Unfortunately, the stones from the top and foot have not survived. On the reverse three circles with gold disks have remained, two with a dark-blue ground and one on green; the others have disappeared. At the top of the cross a fairly thick hinge is pierced by a pin with a pearl at one end.

On the obverse, the branches of the cross are decorated with half-length figures in cloisonné enamel: the Virgin at the top, Saint Demetrius to the left, Saint Nicholas to the right, and below, a rather awkward image of Saint John Chrysostom. All the Greek inscriptions of the names are in red enamel; all the halos are light blue. The Virgin's robe has kept the dark-purple color to be found in the first enamels. Saint Demetrius wears a dark-blue mantle over a red tunic with a lemon-yellow panel. In his hand he holds a red cross. His hair is black, and the enamel of his eyes has disappeared. Saint Nicholas is a white-haired old man, his hair rendered in a bluish smalt. A white stole with two dark-blue crosses is thrown over his dark-blue vestments. He holds a closed book in his left hand. Saint John Chrysostom wears the traditional light-blue alb. His white cassock and stole are decorated with small, dark-blue crosses. His right hand is in the position of benediction, and he holds a closed book in his left hand.

It is to be noted that for the flesh tones of the faces the artist used the traditional pinkish-yellow smalt. The drawing of the figures, whose proportions are a little clumsy, is quite coarse; the heads, wrists, and hands are massive, which is one of the characteristic traits of eighth- and ninth-century Georgian art (of chiseled metal and figures worked in stone). The faces are distinguished by the intensity of their expression; the hair is drawn in accordance with the traditions of early Christian art. This pectoral cross is Georgian work, and was made locally in the late ninth or early tenth century.

THE VIRGIN (*above*) AND SAINTS DEMETRIUS (*left*), NICHOLAS (*right*), AND JOHN CHRYSOSTOM.
OBVERSE OF THE MARTVILI PECTORAL CROSS. FIRST HALF OF 10TH CENTURY

THE BOTKIN COLLECTION RELIQUARY

This oval reliquary in a low-grade silver alloy dates from the end of the ninth century or the first half of the tenth. The cover is in red gold adorned with an enameled motif of the Crucifixion ($3^3/_{16} \times 2^3/_{16}$"). The sides are covered with a stylized vegetable design in niello. On the reverse, there are soldered figures of coarse, late workmanship: busts of the Virgin and Child and the Four Evangelists.

In the center of the obverse, Christ is shown on the cross, in a frontal position with arms horizontal. His head is slightly inclined; the eyes are open, but the right pupil is missing. The artist used a black smalt for the hair and beard. The Saviour wears a long, sleeveless tunic, in light blue with two vertical lemon-yellow bands, which falls down to His heels. Its folds are rendered by clearly drawn, vertical lines. The feet are solid. The turquoise halo bears a red-and-white cross.

The cross itself was probably executed in a dark-green smalt, which has suffered with the passage of time—in fact, it has almost completely disappeared on the horizontal branches. Below the cross there is a Golgotha with the skull of Adam. Above, on either side, are the sun and moon and half-length figures of weeping angels. They wear sky-blue tunics and violet mantles, and their wings are in vivid, contrasting tones.

The Virgin is shown standing in the traditional attitude, with garments of the same blue as Christ's tunic. She has been created with admirable delicacy and harmony.

On the other side there is a standing figure of Saint John, in an equally traditional position,

CRUCIFIXION. COVER OF THE
BOTKIN COLLECTION RELIQUARY.
9TH OR 10TH CENTURY

holding a closed book in his left hand. His sky-blue tunic is striped with red. His cloak falls in folds which cling elegantly to his body; both the general harmony of the proportions and the pictorial character of the drapery are worthy of note.

The faces are all of the same color; here again the pinkish-yellow smalt enabled the artist to render flesh tones faithfully. The inscriptions are in a red smalt and the halos are all in the same turquoise. The rigorous treatment of the figure of Christ, His frontal position on the cross, the coarseness of the drawing, the stylization of the folds on His garment, and the ancient icono-graphical type bear witness to the artist's fidelity to the traditional representation of the subject.

But whereas the Christ is well in the spirit of the eighth and ninth centuries, this is not true of the figures of the Virgin and John the Baptist. These two figures are remarkable for their emotion and vitality, their linear harmony and the grace of their attitudes. They are treated in the style that one sees appearing simultaneously in Byzantium and Georgia at the beginning of the eleventh century. Two artistic currents are thus juxtaposed in the same work of art. In fact, from the end of the tenth century onward a major transformation was taking place in art; ancient traditions had not yet been abandoned, but already the characteristics of a new artistic style were beginning to show themselves.

THE MARTVILI PANAGIA

This medallion takes the form of a cross with rounded arms of equal length, surmounted with a ring adorned with pearls (diameter $1^9/_{16}''$), and edged with a double rank of pearls.

The obverse of the medallion represents *The Descent into Limbo*. Christ, His feet on the two blue-striped gates of Hell, gives His right hand to Adam, who is kneeling on the cover of his sarcophagus. Behind Adam a half-length figure of Eve stretches out her veiled hands.

Christ's cloak seems to float in the wind behind Him. The Saviour has thick black hair and a rounded black beard. Adam is portrayed as an old man. His hair and beard are in a bluish smalt. His costume is composed of alternating light and dark blues.

The figures are in movement, which introduces a certain animation into this traditional composition. The drawing exactly follows the forms. Christ's windblown garments, the two tones used for Adam's clothes, and the style of the drapery enable us to situate this reliquary medallion from Martvili at the end of the tenth or the beginning of the eleventh century.

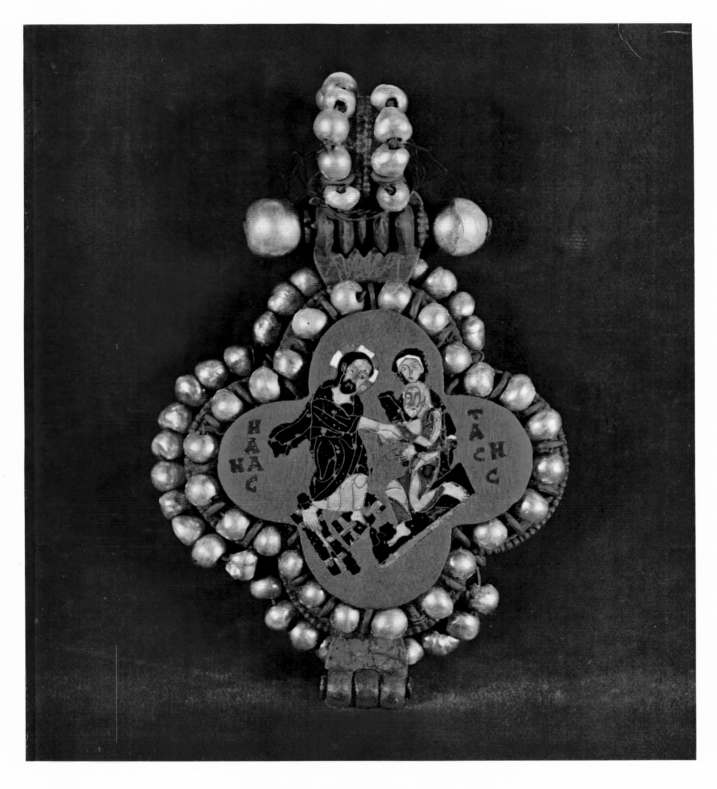

DESCENT INTO LIMBO. OBVERSE OF THE MARTVILI PANAGIA. 10TH OR 11TH CENTURY

GOLD RELIQUARY COVER

The enameled image of Christ seated on a sumptuous throne decorates the gold cover of a silver reliquary. Christ, His right hand held before His breast, is giving a benediction; there is a closed book in His left hand. He has thick black hair, a short, round beard, and wears a dark-blue cloak thrown over a pale-blue tunic. The bands on the sleeves are yellow, as are the two bands at the foot of the tunic. The bare feet rest on a turquoise pedestal decorated on the sides with lapidary inlay motifs.

The oval back of the throne is white and set with small red flowers. Christ is sitting on a green cushion whose ends are decorated with a turquoise band with yellow disks. The yellow binding of the book is set with turquoise stones; two blue clips hold the red pages. Christ's yellow halo bears a cross of white smalt. The blue outline of the halo has largely crumbled away. On the other hand, the face is well preserved; in spite of its small dimensions, its monumental character is striking.

The drawing conveys the forms of the body, rather heavily, perhaps, but faithfully, without aiming at stylization or minute detail. The solemnly seated Christ has a monumental quality. The large head and the generous wrists and feet add to this impression. The artist was probably influenced by the monumental painting of the second half of the tenth century.

CHRIST ENTHRONED. GOLD RELIQUARY COVER

THE BOTKIN COLLECTION GOLD CROSS

This gold cross from the Botkin collection was executed in the eleventh century. It is adorned with an enameled composition of the Crucifixion. A small metal plaque carrying the figure of an Archangel in cloisonné enamel is fixed to the hinge at the top (without this plaque the cross is $6^5/_{16}''$ high).

Christ, on a dark-blue cross, has His eyes closed; His head falls onto His breast and the arms, like the body, are slightly curved. The frontal position proper to cloisonné enamels of the first period is not respected here. A white loin cloth covers the thighs and hips. The feet are nailed separately and rest close together on a small platform, the left foot a little forward. Christ has black hair and a black, slightly forked beard.

Below the cross there is the traditional Golgotha with Adam's skull. Flesh tones are rendered with a remarkably intense smalt.

On the whole, this Crucifixion conforms to the style prevalent in the second half of the eleventh century. All the onlooker's attention is concentrated on the figure of Christ, whose body is shown in perspective, providing a violent contrast with the flat, decorative manner of the previous period.

CRUCIFIXION. OBVERSE OF THE BOTKIN COLLECTION GOLD CROSS. 11TH CENTURY

THE MARTVILI ICON

The famous Martvili icon is executed in repoussé work on a panel of gold. It is decorated with eleven medallions which differ in ornamentation, style, and date of execution.

The central part, a Virgin and Child ($10^5/_8 \times 5^7/_8''$), is worked in gold and nailed onto a silver-gilt surface covered with a luxuriant floral decoration dating from the middle of the seventeenth century. The icon is kept in a decorative reliquary case set with pearls and precious stones. The Child no longer has anything of the severity found in works of the preceding period. He is looking up at His mother, and His whole figure moves toward her. In spite of her traditional position, the Virgin expresses a profound, restrained inner emotion. The two figures are treated in a pictorial relief style. One looks in vain for the delicate tracery of folds, so characteristic of this period's Byzantine art. Instead of the austere, rigorous presentation of the Virgin holding the Messiah, we have a touching image of a simple mother and her son. This is highly important if we are to define the general trend in Georgian art which is, on the whole, less rigidly dogmatic than Byzantine. Another point is worthy of consideration: the clothes of the Virgin and Child are decorated with a plant motif (no corresponding details can be found in similar Byzantine works). These garments are of embroidered cloth, a technique that was still unknown in Orthodox countries before the seventeenth century. Only Western art shows ancient examples of such a treatment of Mary's clothing.

In the top left-hand corner of the frame a small medallion (diameter $^5/_{16}''$) bears the bust of the Apostle Peter. The Apostle's head corresponds to an antique type which was widespread in early Christian art. The hair and beard are gray, the face and hands are a flesh-colored smalt. The outlines of the head and facial details are conveyed with slender gold partitions, the eyebrows and nose with a single thin fillet of gold. The stylized lines of the clothes give a compact expression to the forms. Style and technique lead one to place this enamel medallion of the Apostle Peter in the eighth century.

Immediately below, Christ Pantocrator, His right hand raised in blessing, holds a closed book with yellow binding and red pages in His draped left hand. He wears a sky-blue tunic. This Christ conforms to the traditional type: the emphatic features, the large black pupils of the eyes, and the black beard confer great expressive force on the face. The halo is turquoise blue.

The Virgin, to the right opposite Christ, has both hands raised before her breast, the palms turned outward toward the viewer. Her dark-blue mantle is marked on the head and shoulders with little gold stars and her halo is light blue. Certain traits characteristic of this type of Virgin are to be noted: the elongated neck, the rounded oval head, the arched eyebrows, the large black eyes, and the long, straight nose.

All the names are inscribed with thin fillets of gold.

Above the Virgin, Basil the Great is clad in a blue alb, which offsets his white priestly stole adorned with small crosses. Here again, we have a traditional iconographical type; the long, thick, pointed beard, the black hair, the short, thick eyebrows accentuate the intensity of his expression. The enamel of his forehead has crumbled away. The inscription on the gold background is in brick-red smalt. His right hand is on his breast, while in his left he holds a book bound in brick-red with a blue-green spine.

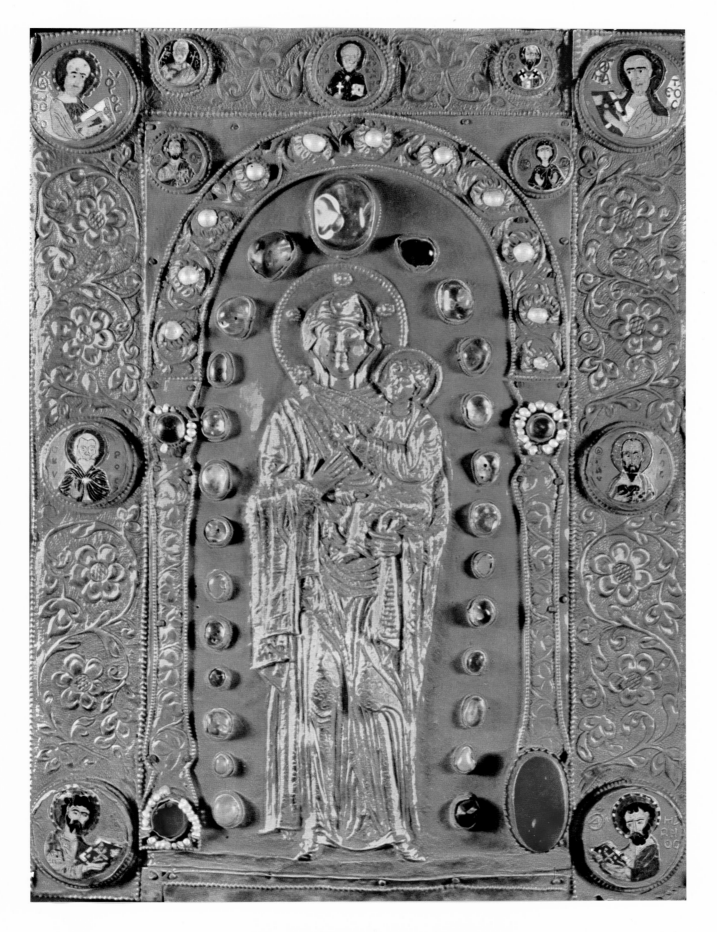

VIRGIN AND CHILD. MARTVILI ICON

MEDALLIONS OF JOHN THE THEOLOGIAN (*left*), SAINT PETER (*above right*), AND CHRIST (*below right*) FROM THE MARTVILI ICON

In the corners of the icon are the Four Evangelists, identical in technique, style, and dimensions. They are obviously the work of a Georgian artist, for they differ strikingly from Byzantine enamels. The scale of colors chosen is distinguished by its particular brightness; contrasting combinations are dominant.

Matthew is shown as an old man. The gray hair and beard and the tunic are in the same pale-blue smalt. The Evangelist is shown in half profile, holding a closed book with white pages bound in brick red. The green halo is also outlined in brick red. The pointed oval of the thin face, and the large

MEDALLIONS OF SAINTS MATTHEW (*right*) AND BASIL (*above left*), AND THE VIRGIN (*below left*)
FROM THE MARTVILI ICON

black eyes give an impression of severity. The inscription is in dark-blue enamel on a white ground.

At the upper left-hand corner the Apostle John, too, is shown in half profile. In his hands is a book bound in brick red, open at a white page on which the characters are not shown. He is an old, bald man with a high, domed forehead, a short gray beard, and black eyebrows. This iconographic type is frequently found in twelfth-century Georgian art, especially in manuscript miniatures. The cloak, the last few gray hairs on the temples, and the gray beard are executed in light-blue enamel. A brick-red band outlined with gold emphasizes the green halo.

TWELFTH-CENTURY GOLD ICON

This icon in gold repoussé work ($3^3/_4 \times 3^{11}/_{32}$") dates from the twelfth century. The Crucifixion is shown in the center of a rectangular plate of gold. The enamel has not kept well; large parts of Christ's left arm and chest have flaked off. The feet are nailed separately, and the left one barely overlaps the edge of the support. The face is finely drawn and has survived in good condition. The white loin cloth is knotted with a red cord whose end hangs down. The weeping Virgin on the left stretches out her right hand to her Son and holds her head in the other. Behind the Mother of God stands Mary Cleophas in a stricken attitude, her head bowed.

To the right of the cross are John and the centurion Longinus. In accordance with tradition, John is resting his head sadly in his right hand. The centurion, with a shield in his left hand, his eyes raised to heaven, is clothed in the usual uniform.

Above, to either side of the cross, there are two angels with multicolored wings. Flesh tones are rendered with a pale-pink smalt. The lines follow exactly the forms of the bodies. The drapery is harmoniously executed with slender gold partitions. Here and there it is arranged in a herringbone pattern, a characteristic trait of twelfth-century cloisonné enamels. Moreover, the expression of profound sadness on every face, and the fact that Christ is shown slightly in profile, turned to the left, permit us to place this enameled icon of the Crucifixion in the very last years of the twelfth century.

CRUCIFIXION. ENAMELED GOLD ICON. 12TH CENTURY

CROSS
FROM THE KATSKHI ICON

The icon of the Saviour from Katskhi incorporates a small enameled cross ($4^1/_{16} \times 2^3/_8''$) fixed to the binding of a closed book held by Christ. The cross itself is badly damaged, for most of the enamel has flaked off, leaving only the right hand of Christ. The right arm of the piece is also in poor condition. The style and technique of this cross place it among the first Georgian enamels. It is adorned at the top with a medallion (diameter $^3/_8''$) containing a bust of the Archangel Michael.

The medallion placed at the foot of the cross, an Archangel without an orb, seems a direct replica of the one above, for the same colors are used in the garments, wings, and halo. The facial features, wavy hair, eyes, and other details are treated in the same style, and in both cases the background is dark green. The Archangel wears a square red cross on his chest.

On the left arm, the Virgin is shown in an attitude of prayer, her arm raised against a dark-blue ground. Here the usual cape is replaced with a dark-purple veil that covers the head. The garments are executed in a translucent green enamel. The drapery is coarsely rendered with straightforward drawing. The Virgin's face is distinguished by its oval form, long and very emphatic arched black eyebrows, enlarged black pupils, fine, straight nose, small mouth, and long neck. The image has great spiritual quality and inimitable beauty. Behind the Virgin we see her initial in Georgian traced with a fine fillet of gold.

This cross carries a rich checkerboard decoration. Such treatment was used for a long time in Byzantine and Georgian art, especially in enamelwork. The piece can be dated in the eighth or ninth century.

QUEEN TAMARA'S CROSS

Queen Tamara's pectoral cross, formerly kept in the monastery of Khobi, is now the pride of the Georgian National Museum of Fine Arts. This small folding object ($2^3/_4 \times 1^9/_{16}''$) must be considered among the masterpieces of the Georgian jeweler's craft. The obverse is set with four semicylindrical Indian emeralds. Five rubies are set at the extremities and in the center of the cross. The decoration is completed with four large pear-shaped pearls set diagonally. Two other pearls are fixed on either side of the hinge that links the cross to its openwork chain. On the reverse there is an inscription in ancient Georgian, which confirms that the cross belonged to the illustrious Queen Tamara who reigned from 1184–1212.

It was definitely not until after the death of the Queen that the cross was placed in a specially made gold reliquary. This case consists of two wings. When closed, the obverse shows the Saviour in benediction, holding a closed book in His left hand. The face was entirely repainted in the nineteenth century. The background is worked in niello.

On the reverse, only four enamel medallions have survived, Byzantine work of the twelfth century. A large medallion originally occupied the center, but the enamel has completely crumbled away, and a half-length figure of Saint Basil was painted in its place. In the four corners there are busts of John Chrysostom, Gregory the Theologian, Ignatius Upholder of the Faith, and John the Evangelist. These figures have taken on a vitreous quality; they were probably darkened as a result of the cleaning carried out in the nineteenth century.

At the top, there is a medallion of the Virgin, her hands on her breast, with her palms outturned. Another medallion shows Nicholas the Miraculous giving the blessing. Clothed in a priest's alb, he has a blue chasuble over his shoulders with a stole marked with crosses. This was a current iconographical type in tenth- and eleventh-century Byzantine art.

Saint George wears an emerald-green cape. He is shown as an adolescent with curly hair and fine features. Saint Demetrius is a young man with hair swept back from a round face. He wears a brick-red cape and a white tunic, and there is a blue cross on his yellow stole; his halo is turquoise.

The cloisonné enamels of this diptych present considerable artistic interest. All the Greek inscriptions are in brick-red smalt on a gold ground. These enamels are remarkable for their sure execution and the harmonious combinations of colors, characteristic of Byzantine art at the end of the tenth century and the beginning of the eleventh.

 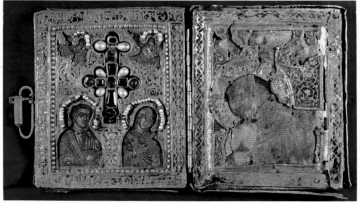

EXTERIOR (*left*) AND INTERIOR (*right*) OF THE RELIQUARY FOR QUEEN TAMARA'S CROSS

The interior of the reliquary contains a niche intended to hold the cross. On either side there are half-length figures of weeping angels, and at the foot are half-length figures of the Virgin and Saint John in the traditional positions. The image of the Virgin is partially damaged, especially the face. On the other hand, the painting of Saint John has been preserved in good condition in its original form. This work, which dates from the first half of the thirteenth century, is of the greatest artistic importance.

The other panel of the reliquary shows Christ in the tomb. Unfortunately, all the paint has flaked off this part.

Around the outside edge of the case one can read an inscription reproducing exactly the inscription on the Queen's cross. However, the last words of the inscription on the lower edge have been erased deliberately. From what remains of these letters, we can decipher the words: *Aid me, Eristav Tsotné, and George the son of my brother*. The *in memoriam* inscription invokes Queen Tamara's cross and reproduces her prayer word for word. It is no doubt for this reason that the name of Tsotné Dadiani, who had no scruples in appropriating the illustrious ruler's prayer for himself, was carefully effaced.

Georgian cloisonné enamels give an autochthonous image of their historical evolution until the eleventh century. The art of enamelwork had its own style and processes which appeared at the

OBVERSE OF QUEEN TAMARA'S CROSS

beginning of the feudal period. But in the early eleventh century the cultural and artistic life of Georgia became closely linked with the cultural and artistic centers of Byzantium, whether in the Second Empire (Constantinople) or at Mount Athos, Antioch, Bythnia, etc. In this connection it is impossible to exaggerate the importance of the Georgian monastery of Romanus at Constantinople (eleventh century), the Georgian community in the monastery of Saint Khors (Kahrie-Jami), and above all, the Athonite monastery of Iviron (tenth century).

Miniatures in ancient manuscripts preserve outstanding evidence of Byzantine influence. The cultural link with Byzantium took place with the help of erudite translators like Evfrimij and Giorgi Sviatogortsi of the School of Athens, Efrim Mtsiré of the School of the Black Mountain near Antioch, Ioann Petritsi and Arseni of Iq'alto from the School of Petritsion (the Georgian monastery at Bochkovi in Bulgaria) among others.

However, the quest for closer links between Georgian religious culture and Greek culture, the will to equal the Greeks in all things and maintain the purity of the Orthodox faith, and the assimilation of the achievements of Byzantine civilization did not stifle the Georgian feeling of national dignity. With the words of one of their representatives on Mount Sinai, Monk John (late tenth century), the Georgians proclaimed the equality between their language and Greek: "The Georgian tongue and the Greek tongue are two friendly sisters, like Martha and Mary."

THE TSILKANI ICON

The Tsilkani icon was no doubt made in western Georgia. The Child is shown in a slightly oblique position, but His gaze is fixed on the viewer. His left foot is placed a little forward. The Child gives a blessing with His right hand, and holds a scroll in the other. The Virgin's left hand passes under the Child's armpit, and this detail sets the composition in a place apart in iconography. On either side in the background stand the Archangels Michael and Gabriel, with orbs and scepters. All the garments are red; those of the Child, in golden ochre, stand out luminously against the rest. The angels' sashes are decorated with precious stones. On the lower part of the frame an inscription in ancient Georgian tells us that the painting was ordered by Archbishop Bartholomew of Tsilkani.

The icon and its inscription were executed cold on a wax emulsion. The faces are distinguished by generous, thick strokes. Lighting is arranged by the use of heavily whitened flesh tones touched with pink on the cheeks. The drawing of eyes and noses, eyebrows and mouths is dry and stylized. One can conclude that the work is related to eight- and ninth-century Oriental models, though the piece itself was not ordered until the turn of the tenth or eleventh century. In accordance with the ancient tradition of Georgian painting, the icon ($27^9/_{16} \times 22^1/_{16}''$) is painted on a hollowed-out panel.

The heads of the Madonna and Child are circled with precious halos. The Virgin's, in gold, is in five parts. The decoration is remarkably fine and surprisingly accomplished. The Child's halo is entirely executed on gold. The enamel ground carries a scroll pattern, inside which there are small, stylized flowers on a bright-green ground.

The upper frame of the icon carries the Warrior Saints: Theodore Tiro and Theodore Stratelates. The two saints resemble one another so closely that only certain details of their clothing and their magnificent weapons enable one to distinguish between them. The torso of Theodore Stratelates is portrayed on a larger scale. In his right hand he holds the lance with which he slew the dragon. Theodore Tiro, like Stratelates, carries an oval shield marked with a dragon. The two saints share the same fine features, the slightly elongated oval of their faces, black, pointed beards, and thick, curly, black hair.

The two other medallions show the Healer Saints, Damian and Pantaleon, holding boxes of medicine. Damian is a mature man, Pantaleon young. Both are dressed as patricians.

The enamels of the Tsilkani icon have considerable artistic value, and are set apart by their masterly execution. They concentrate mainly on decoration, and stylization of forms. A system of polychromy, based on the combination of intensely luminous complementary tones, dominates everywhere. Moreover, the Tsilkani medallions reveal a taste for minute detail which contributes precisely to the striking distribution of the various tones. The drawing of the faces is indeed stylized, but this in no way diminishes the work's expressive strength.

VIRGIN AND CHILD WITH ARCHANGELS. TSILKANI ICON. 10TH OR 11TH CENTURY

ICONS OF THE HOLY FEASTS

The series of icons on the theme of The Holy Feasts comes from the Botkin collection and dates from the end of the twelfth century. It consisted of eleven compositions; only *The Annunciation* was missing.

Three of the eleven enameled panels were restored to Georgia in 1923 and placed in the National Museum: *The Presentation at the Temple, The Raising of Lazarus,* and *The Apparition of the Holy Spirit.* The fate of the others is unknown.

While they were perhaps not all the work of the same artist, all the Holy Feasts came from the same workshop. There are no explanatory inscriptions.

The Presentation at the Temple, The Raising of Lazarus, and *The Apparition of the Holy Spirit* are treated against complex architectural backgrounds to which the artist gave great importance. Elements drawn from Georgian national architecture predominate in these three scenes, taking the place of the traditional, conventionalized architectural motifs that had begun to play a considerable role in Byzantine and Georgian art during the late twelfth century. The architectural content in *The Presentation at the Temple* consists, in the center of the composition, of a Georgian church with the typical drum surmounted by a conical cupola crowned with a cross. The windows in the drum of the cupola also have a characteristic native form.

In *The Raising of Lazarus* one notices an obvious effort to convey depth. Christ, surrounded by apostles, is shown against a gray-violet background of mountains, and Lazarus stands out against a

THE PRESENTATION AT THE TEMPLE. 12TH CENTURY

THE RAISING OF LAZARUS. 12TH CENTURY

THE APPARITION OF THE HOLY SPIRIT. 12TH CENTURY

doorway, beyond which one can see another gray-violet peak. The conventional architecture of the background is arranged between these two mountains. It is, in fact, the arrangement of natural and architectural landscapes that gives the composition its depth.

This succinctly expressed desire to represent space is a new artistic phenomenon which does not appear before the end of the twelfth century, and so enables us to establish a precise date for this series of works.

The Presentation at the Temple corresponds to the traditional iconographical arrangement. The Mother of God holds the Child, shown in fullface in a striped tunic, in her arms. Joseph follows the Virgin, and carries a basket with two white doves. On the other side, the old man Simeon holds out his draped hands. Beyond Simeon stands the prophetess Anne. Between these figures, in the foreground, stands a candlestick.

The movement of the figures is harmonious and rhythmic, without jerkiness. In all three compositions the heads are enlarged, giving the figures a certain heaviness. The faces have strikingly intense expressions, accentuated by the large black pupils of the eyes. The drawing of the drapery folds is particularly effective, with its delicate execution and rhythmic, pictorial arrangement which follows the general direction of movement of the figures and magnificently suggests the veiled forms.

In Georgian art, such an arrangement of drapery already heralds ornamental stylization, which is not to be found before the end of the twelfth century.

THE KORTSHELI ICON

The style of its execution and the sensitivity with which traditional themes are treated relates the Kortsheli icon to the Holy Feasts images. It is decorated with cloisonné enamel figures.

On the reverse an inscription tells us that in 1652 the old panel painted with a bust of the Virgin was replaced with a new plaque showing the Saviour in benediction (from which most of the paint has since flaked off). This icon was placed in a silver case adorned with images of the Twelve Prophets and two kneeling figures: the donor and his wife. According to the inscription, the case dates from 1640.

What *has* survived is the partly damaged, magnificent gold covering ($7^7/_8 \times 6^5/_{16}''$) laden with enamel figures. The icon is enriched with a blue enamel ground against which young white shoots rise vertically, enclosing flowers topped with red buds in their oval scroll pattern. The crown is in keeping with this motif; it is slightly concave and set with small crosses, alternately blue and red on a white ground, and small circles with red palm motifs on a turquoise ground. A checkerboard pattern is placed diagonally around the border of the background.

The Assumption of the Virgin is represented in the center of the upper part of the covering. On either side are two apocryphal scenes. An angel carries the Apostle John to the Virgin's deathbed in Jerusalem; another does the same with Mark. These figures, seen in half-length, are surrounded by floating, wavy clouds, rendered in pale and cobalt blue.

The scene of *The Assumption* is worthy of further attention, for whereas it adheres to the established rules of iconography, it is treated with a certain dramatic intensity. The Virgin is lying on a red funeral bed draped in red and pale green. Christ receives the soul of His mother, while weeping angels descend from the heavens on either side. To the far side of the head of the bed stands the Apostle Andrew, shown as an old man, his head bowed in sadness. In the foreground opposite Andrew, the Apostle Peter holds the incense burner, while the Apostle Paul kneels at the foot of the bed. The other apostles are arranged in two pictorial groups that convey profound emotion and sadness.

In the center of the lower part of the frame we have *The Birth of the Virgin*, flanked by towers on either side. Anne is on a white bed draped in green; at her feet two women bring gifts. *The Bathing of the Child* was represented in the foreground, but this has been badly damaged. A fragment of the Child's bed, near Anne's elbow, has survived.

To the left of this composition there was originally a half-length figure of Saint Barbara, now completely lost. All we have is the Greek inscription of the name. Beside Saint Barbara, in the corner, the image of Saint Catherine has also disappeared, but again the Greek inscription is clearly legible. The latter image has been replaced with the bust of a male saint.

At the center of the left side of the covering we have the scene of *The Annunciation*. The Archangel Gabriel, his right hand raised, announces the good news. A ray of light sparks out from a blue hemisphere to fall on the Virgin. Behind her, in the background, there is a tower-shaped building. Mary has her right hand raised to her breast, palm turned outward, and holds in the other a spindle around which a crimson thread is wound.

To the right, in the center, stand the Virgin's parents, Joachim and Anne. The figure of Anne is missing. Between these scenes around the frame are pairs of six-winged cherubim and seraphim.

In spite of its relationship with the composition of the Holy Feasts, the Kortsheli icon is later in date. The dramatic intensity of the scene of *The Assumption* shows a style that appears in Byzantium, Georgia, and the Balkans in the thirteenth century.

From the comparative study of the Byzantine and Georgian enamels in the collection of the Georgian National Museum of Fine Arts, we can conclude that in the Middle Ages there existed two main artistic currents. In the eleventh century, Georgian enamelwork, which had developed on the basis of an ancient national art, came under Byzantine influences. After this, there appeared a whole series of works in cloisonné enamel which are to be counted among the finest of their time, and which concede nothing to Byzantine work in the quality of their execution. Parallel to this, many key pieces of Georgian cloisonné enamelwork remained faithful to ancient national traditions and kept their local characteristics over a long period.

CHRIST IN BENEDICTION. KORTSHELI ICON. 17TH CENTURY

THE GELATI ICON

MEDALLION OF THE SACRED THRONE FROM THE GELATI ICON

The icon of the Saviour from Gelati ($15^3/_4 \times 11^{13}/_{16}''$) includes six cloisonné enamels of which one, Saint George, is Greek and the others are Georgian. These enamel medallions are set around the gold frame, on which the niello ornament reveals a highly developed decorative sense. Christ's slightly convex golden halo is covered with a delicate, complex pattern. The organization of this decoration recalls that often found on eleventh-century engraved altar railings. The cross on the halo is in white enamel; against this background we see a plant motif and cloisonné settings intended to hold precious stones.

The Saviour is represented in Majesty, giving the blessing with His right hand, while the left holds a preciously bound book. Christ's face, especially the left side, has been badly damaged. The original work has not survived, but the execution and style of the existing painting point to a mid-seventeenth-century restoration.

The top center medallion represents the Sacred Throne, which supports a crowned cross, a sponge, and a lance. To the left of the figure of Christ is the Apostle Peter wearing a pale-green tunic with a red stripe. His cloak is bicolored. The curly grizzled hair, the beard, and eyebrows are in light-blue enamel; the halo is pale turquoise.

To the right of Christ, is the Apostle Paul in a deep-blue tunic with a yellow and brick-red stripe and a light-green cloak. The figure remains faithful to the traditional type: black hair, high brow, thick eyebrows, large black eyes, and black beard. The Evangelist Luke is shown as a middle-aged man, with divided beard and wavy hair. The dark eyes and thick eyebrows faithfully render the iconographical type. The smalt used to convey the flesh tones of the faces and hands is extremely translucent in parts, as is the enamel used for the dark-green halos of Paul and Luke.

The outlines, executed with gold partitions, are drawn without rigor, and in places are even confused and lacking in firmness. However, the ease of execution and the painterly nature of the composition are noteworthy. Furthermore, whereas each figure closely follows the traditional iconographical type, the artist has endowed each one with an individuality that approaches portraiture, an indication of the level reached by Georgian art at the middle of the twelfth century.

CHRIST IN MAJESTY. GELATI ICON

While this group of enamels does not equal Greek productions in technical skill or quality of execution, the manner and the glowing colors, the richness and audacity of color combinations, give the works their own particular beauty. The creator of these medallions was not familiar with severity, understatement, systematic treatment of detail, or ornamental stylization of drapery, all of which typify those Georgian and Byzantine enamels influenced by Greek work.

The medallion of Saint George, placed at the foot of the frame, cannot be classed with the group just studied. The saint's mantle is light green, and he carries a blue cross in his right hand. The features of the young saint are executed with outstanding skill and expressed with great severity. The pinkish-yellow tones of the face and hands are tinged with gray. The halo is blue and there is a brick-red inscription on the gold ground. This is beyond doubt Byzantine work of the eleventh century.

The Georgian enamels, the halo, and the nominative inscription close to Christ's head are dated in a niello annotation mentioning the donor, a powerful chancellor of the late eleventh and early twelfth century. This fact is of the greatest importance, for it enables us to establish a chronology for the Georgian enamels related to the Gelati works—that is, those from Tsalendgika, Khobi, and Jumati.

MEDALLIONS OF SAINTS PAUL (*left*) AND PETER (*right*) FROM THE GELATI ICON

MEDALLIONS OF SAINTS LUKE (*left*) AND GEORGE (*right*) FROM THE GELATI ICON

THE TSALENDGIKA ICON

The icon of the Saviour from Tsalendgika was decorated with ten enameled medallions of the same style and period. One was already missing in 1913. Today, the covering of the icon is mounted on a new panel. Two medallions, showing Christ and John the Baptist, are fixed to the upper part of the frame. The other medallions and rosettes are exhibited separately among the general collection of cloisonné enamels (pages 16, 20, and 21). The icon is executed in repoussé work ($28^9/_{16}$ × $20^{11}/_{16}$"); the center is a leaf of enameled silver. Christ Pantocrator is shown in half-length on a decorative ground. His head is ringed by a halo and His hidden left hand holds a closed book.

The frame is composed of four sheets of gilt-silver, richly decorated in niello. Since the panel on which the metal was fixed had been eaten by worms, the face of Christ was repainted on a new panel, cut according to the outline, and inset separately.

John the Baptist is shown in supplication. His tousled hair and beard are black, his clothes in two tones of blue.

The drawing in these enamels, executed with thin gold bands, is uneven in quality, and in some parts loose, but the over-all ease of the lines relates the two medallions to the Gelati icon enamels. The relationship is accentuated by the individual nature of the figures, showing a tendency toward portraiture. If one compares Georgian enamels of this group with Byzantine work, one can see that Georgian artists were continuing the traditions of the earliest enamels.

MEDALLIONS OF CHRIST (*left*) AND JOHN THE BAPTIST (*right*) FROM THE TSALENDGIKA ICON

CHRIST PANTOCRATOR. TSALENDGIKA ICON

THE KHOBI ICON

The enamels on the half-length *Deisis* from Khobi belong to the corpus of Georgian cloisonné enamels. The icon of the Virgin ($21^{11}/_{16} \times 16^{15}/_{16}"$) was executed in repoussé on a plate of silver. The frame is composed of four leaves covered with a carefully studied decoration. The form of the motif varies from one scrolled section to the next. Medallions are set between these independent decorative elements.

The half-length figure of the Virgin is in fairly high relief, emphasized by the folds of the drapery, arranged almost horizontally on the right shoulder, from which other folds seem to fall obliquely. The folds over the left arm set off the modeling of the left hand. The forms of the hands, particularly the fingers, are rendered with masterly delicacy.

An inscription in ancient Georgian runs along the lower edge of the border of the icon. It alludes to the Emperor Leon, whose titles are not listed. Specialists are in unanimous agreement that the Emperor in question is Leon III, who reigned between approximately 957 and 987. The text of the inscription—*Most pure Mother of God, intercede with Christ for the soul of the Emperor Leon*—implies that it was made after the death of the Emperor.

On the obverse the lower edge is covered with a thin band of gilt repoussé work, probably dating from the sixteenth century. This band was removed to reveal two other inscriptions of different dates. The first must have been contemporary with the one mentioning Leon III. The text is slightly damaged but can easily be reconstructed: *Most pure Mother of God, accord thy grace to Mariamme, Empress of empresses, and her son Constantine, Emperor of emperors!* The Emperor Constantine to whom allusion is made here preceded Leon III on the throne and reigned from approximately 893 to 922. The covering of this icon therefore dates from before the death of Leon III. Unfortunately, the original painting has not survived and a nineteenth-century restoration seriously altered the work.

THE VIRGIN. KHOBI ICON

THE KHOBI DEISIS. *From left ... AND JOHN THE BAPTIST*

The second inscription can be dated in the second half of the thirteenth century. Palaeographically it is absolutely similar to the inscription just mentioned, and cites two goldsmiths, Mikel and Daniel, who renovated the icon of the Virgin and were probably responsible for the enamel figures. Another inscription on the silvered reverse face of the icon tells us that during the reign of David, Emperor of emperors (1243–1293), the icon was decorated with fervor and the back covered with metal, in gratitude for the favors granted by the Virgin.

The upper part of the frame shows the *Deisis*: in the center is a medallion with the image of Christ, and at either corner are medallions of the Virgin and John the Baptist. All these enameled figures have the same dimensions (diameter $1^9/_{16}''$). The names, written in Georgian, are in red enamel on a gold ground. The drawing is sometimes uneven and careless; the coloring of the garments is characterized by a range of light tints in which the juxtaposition of complementary tones predominates.

Christ, blessing with His right hand, holds a book bound in red and yellow in the other. His face, neck, hand, hair, beard, and tunic are executed in the same color—a little darker, however, for the hair and beard. The cross on the yellow halo outlined in red is filled in with a dark-red smalt.

The Virgin is shown in an attitude of prayer. Her thick black eyebrows, the large black pupils, the slightly elongated oval of her face, and the bright lips give the figure great expressive force. John the Baptist is also shown in prayer. His black hair stands out sharply against the yellow halo emphasized by a red outline. The thick black hair and beard, the short, thick eyebrows, and large black pupils convey the traditional archetype of the Precursor.

78

MEDALLIONS FROM THE KHOBI ICON.

From left to bottom: SAINTS MATTHEW, LUKE, MARK, ANDREW, PAUL, AND PETER

The Apostle Peter is seen in fullface. The entire figure, except for the eyebrows, which are thick and black, is treated with a gray-violet smalt of varying intensities. The bright-green halo, without a contrasting outline, offsets this monochrome figure. The Apostle Paul, too, is shown in fullface.

The lower frame of the icon carries three evangelists—Matthew, Mark, and Luke—seen in a frontal position. Matthew is shown as an old man, his right hand on his breast and the left holding a book bound in red. His halo is pale green outlined in red. The face, hair, and beard are rendered in varied tones of gray-violet smalt. Saint Mark is a mature man with black hair and a short, slightly rounded black beard. His yellow halo has a red outline. His draped left hand holds a closed red book, and the other is raised in blessing. His garments are pale green. Saint Luke is also shown giving benediction, and holds a white scroll in his left hand. He has a green halo outlined in red.

The Apostle Andrew is represented in the same attitude as Saint Luke. His yellow halo outlined in red contrasts strongly with his dark garments. The Apostle is shown as an old man with gray hair and short pointed beard rendered in light-blue smalt. The black eyebrows and pupils stress the severity of this representation.

THE JUMATI ICON

Six of the ten medallions that decorated this icon have been destroyed. The half-length figure of Christ is shown in fullface (diameter $2^3/_4''$). The right hand is raised in benediction, while the left holds a closed book with white pages, bound in red. His garments are blue and the white cross of the halo is rimmed with a band of red dotted with white. The face is freely drawn; thick eyebrows and black pupils increase the expression's intensity.

Saint Demetrius is also shown in fullface, holding a naked sword in his right hand and its sheath in the other. He is a young man with thick, curly hair. His black eyebrows and large eyes gazing to one side confer a certain gravity on his figure.

The medallion enameled with a bust of Saint Luke (diameter $2^{15}/_{16}''$) is also of Georgian workmanship. The Evangelist has his right hand clasped to his breast, while the other holds a closed book bound in yellow with red stones in the corners and a rhomboidal green stone in the center.

In contrast to the careless execution and the pictorial freedom of the drawing, the choice and disposition of colors, mainly bright tints, are extremely rich, particularly in the medallion of Saint Theodore. The enameled smalt possesses remarkable purity and the colors are often translucent, particularly the emerald greens. The violet-tinged smalt that characterizes this group of enamels is used exclusively to render flesh tones.

Unfortunately, in some of these works the polishing leaves much to be desired; the blacks are covered with tiny spots and in some places, especially around the edges, the smalt has split and flaked away.

MEDALLIONS OF CHRIST (*above left*) AND SAINTS DEMETRIUS (*above right*), THEODORE (*below left*), AND LUKE (*below right*) FROM THE JUMATI ICON

ICONS OF SAINT GEORGE

Two icons representing Saint George are to be placed among the last productions of Georgian enamelwork. One shows him slaying the dragon, the other rescuing the maiden. These two icons were returned to Georgia in 1923. They are almost of equal size ($5^{11}/_{16} \times 4^{9}/_{16}''$; $6^{11}/_{16} \times 5^{1}/_{8}''$) and can be assigned to the same period and artist.

The saint, in military uniform, is riding a white horse. His cloak, fixed with a clasp on his chest, floats in the wind. The two themes are treated in accordance with the text of the life of Saint George which describes in detail the Miracle of the Dragon.

Apart from some insignificant differences, the artist has used the same assortment of colors for the two compositions. Saint George is almost identical in the two icons.

In the first, Saint George is slaying the dragon; he plunges his lance into the animal's open mouth. The ample folds of his cape, perhaps rather conventional, expressively convey the sense of movement suggested by the whole scene. The horse raises its forelegs; the dragon writhes around its hind legs.

At the top, the Right Hand of God gives a benediction.

SAINT GEORGE SLAYING THE DRAGON. FIRST HALF OF 15TH CENTURY

The second icon shows the saint riding in triumph. His lance is pointing upward and he holds the reins in his left hand. In front of the saint, a young girl wearing the sumptuous dress of a daughter of a Byzantine emperor leads the conquered dragon, which has a collar around its neck.

There are inscriptions in Greek and Georgian on both icons, the Greek in red enamel and the Georgian in a dark-blue smalt. These give us a solid basis on which to situate these two icons in the first half of the fifteenth century and consider them as the last manifestations of the art of cloisonné enameling in Georgia.

SAINT GEORGE RESCUING THE EMPEROR'S DAUGHTER. FIRST HALF OF 15TH CENTURY

BYZANTINE ENAMELS

THE SHEMOSHMEDI ICON

The enameled icon of Shemoshmedi ($5^1/_8 \times 7^1/_{16}''$), set in a silver triptych of late workmanship, is one of the finest specimens of Byzantine cloisonné enamel and is conserved in the Georgian National Museum of Fine Arts.

The enameled figures are executed on small plates of gold set into a silver coffer ($3^1/_2 \times 3^1/_2''$). This coffer was placed in a case decorated with filigree and colored stones. The frame carries a zigzag checkerboard pattern, which has survived only in part. The corners of the three square panels above and below are adorned with a floral motif identical in color and design.

In the top center, Christ has His right hand raised in blessing; in the other He holds a closed book bound in yellow. The enamel of the halo has flaked off. The facial features are executed with delicate mastery, and are highly expressive.

To Christ's right is the Apostle Peter, with wavy hair, rounded beard, and eyebrows all rendered in a pale-blue smalt. The tunic and mantle are treated in alternating tones of blue.

The Apostle Paul is on the left of Christ. His long, oval face, short black hair, pointed beard, and black pupils provide an admirable expression of the iconographical type as it became fixed in Byzantine art. His clothing is executed in the same tints as the garments of the Apostle Peter.

The Annunciation and *The Descent into Limbo* fill the central part of the icon. The Virgin, with her head bowed, listens attentively to the Messenger Angel. In her left hand she holds a spindle with a white thread, instead of the traditional crimson. Her right hand is held to her breast and the expression on her face conveys surprise and piety. The Archangel Gabriel is represented in rapid movement, his right hand held out toward the Virgin to announce the good news, his left holding a staff. His clothes are treated in two shades of blue. The Virgin, who is depicted with greater severity, is clad in dark blue. This scene is remarkable for its harmonious proportions and supple movement. The fine features and magnificently drawn black eyebrows and pupils, the straight nose and long neck, stress the soft feminine nature of the face.

In *The Descent into Limbo*, Christ is carried along in swift movement. He is standing, legs apart, on the gates of Hell and his cloak floats in the wind. His attitude is almost an exact reproduction of that of the Archangel. He is helping old Adam out of his sarcophagus. Eve, in an attitude of prayer in the background, holds out her hands to Christ. In the left-hand corner David and Solomon are emerging from their tombs.

Christ is wearing a tunic over which a cloak is thrown. His halo is blue with a white cross. The foot of the tunic is decorated with vertical yellow stripes. The Saviour carries a red scroll in his left hand. Adam's hair, beard, and mustache are in a light-blue smalt and his garments are treated in the same colors as Christ's. Eve is wearing a purple-violet mantle. Solomon is a young man wearing the costume of an emperor and David is a gray-bearded old man, a crown on his head. The sarcophagus is depicted in two colors.

In the center of the lower tier there is the great martyr Pantaleon portrayed as an adolescent. He holds a lancet in his right hand and a casket in the other. His tunic and mantle are light blue, and his turquoise halo is rimmed with brick red.

To his right, also with a turquoise halo, Cosmas, with black hair and a short black beard, wears a dark-blue cloak and a pale-blue tunic. He holds a scroll in each hand. The figure to the left of Saint Pantaleon is Saint Damian. His hair is black and his beard short; his right hand is raised in benediction, while his left holds a mortar with a glass lid.

The inscriptions are in brick-red enamel on a gold ground. The two tones of blue in the clothing are enriched here and there with garnet red. The enamel smalt is outstandingly pure in tone and translucency. The use of thin partitions for even the most minute details gives proof of a highly advanced technique. The presence of two tones of smalt in the garments, the elegant drawing of the drapery folds, the uniformly violet-tinged yellow of the flesh, the care taken in polishing, and the harmonious interplay of colors allow us to date these compositions at the end of the tenth century.

SHEMOSHMEDI ICON. *From top, left to right:* SAINT PETER, CHRIST, SAINT PAUL, THE DESCENT
INTO LIMBO, THE ANNUNCIATION, SAINTS COSMAS, PANTALEON, AND DAMIAN.
IOTH CENTURY

SAINT PETER FROM THE GELATI ICON

This Byzantine work, taken from the Gelati icon of the Virgin, dates from the second half of the thirteenth century. It is a small enamel plaque showing a standing, semiprofile figure of Saint Peter giving a blessing with his right hand and holding a scroll in the other. His tunic is light, his cloak dark blue; he has curly gray hair and a round, curled beard. The hair, beard, and eyebrows are executed in pale-blue enamel. The enlarged black pupils gazing to the right emphasize the severity of the Saint's expression. Unfortunately, the enamel of the halo and neck has crumbled away.

The figure is distinguished by its harmonious proportions. The drawing of the folds of the garments, though a little tenuous, renders exactly the conventional arrangement of drapery, noticeably in the stylized, decorative treatment, and the disposition of the folds in a herringbone pattern, particularly on the chest. This part of the composition is treated in tones of blue. The halo is dark green outlined with brick red.

The Botkin collection includes an analogous work showing Saint Peter, but it is Georgian in execution. The Apostle's name is written in Georgian and Greek. However, the two compositions present a certain number of differences in style. On the Georgian plaque the coloring of the garments is brighter and more strongly contrasted, and the drapery is treated more pictorially, without the hatching characteristic of Byzantine enamels.

SAINT PETER. ENAMELED PLAQUE FROM THE GELATI ICON.
SECOND HALF OF 13TH CENTURY

THE KHAKHULI TRIPTYCH

The world-famous Khakhuli triptych is one of the principal examples of Georgian decorative art. The work is complex in structure and incorporates elements from many different periods. The quality of the repoussé work, the cloisonné enamels of different styles and periods, the chiseled stones and gems that adorn the triptych make it one of the most interesting specimens of medieval Georgian art.

The entire triptych is covered with richly decorated sheets of repoussé metal; the center is in red gold, the side panels in an alloy of silver and gold gilded over fire. As these panels were conceived and executed together, they constitute a homogeneous decorative ensemble. The metal covering of the triptych has undergone no major restoration.

The enameled plaques and medallions of the Saints are the parts of the icon that interest us most. They differ in date, style, and technique, and are fixed to the covering in special bezels made to fit them exactly. The repoussé surface serves as a background and therefore plays a purely auxiliary role. However, each and every element has such considerable artistic value that they can all be considered independent works of art without detracting from the unity of the work as a whole. Even the repoussé inscription in ancient Georgian, placed on the lower edge of the two side panels, is integrated into the over-all composition.

Including the side panels ($45^5/_{16} \times 20^1/_2''$), the Khakhuli triptych measures $78^3/_4''$ across and $57^7/_8''$ high. It is a shrine made to hold a *Deisis* icon of the Virgin in Supplication in its center.

The icon itself was enormously popular in Georgia. For centuries it was watched over attentively by the monarch and the Church. It disappeared in the course of the collectors' plundering expeditions in 1859 and was only restored to Georgia in 1923.

Of the original triptych, conceived in the first half of the tenth century, we have the decoration of the side panels and a few enameled fragments. It was no doubt as a result of Turkish incursions into southwest Georgia that the icon was transferred to the monastery of Gelati by David the Builder (1106–1125). His successor, Dimitri I (1125–1146) ordered the execution of a new shrine with side panels, which has come down to us in its original state. It is the work of three artists who worked separately, but in terms of a single master plan.

The background of the triptych is covered with stylized leaves that seem to spring from the lower part of the frame. The motif resembles a stem that divides to form single or double decorative scrolls, each enclosing stylized relief foliage with scalloped edges, like acanthus leaves. Although there is only one decorative motif, three different manners can be traced in its execution.

The decoration of the right-hand panel has a clear-cut form; it is not overloaded with detail, nor does it cover completely the smooth surface of the metal. The relief is regular, as are the transitions from relief elements to smooth surface, which gives the decoration its pictorial character. The central part of each leaf motif is concave, and as with acanthus leaves, the edges are curved outward. The entire surface is worked in detail on the obverse.

The artist responsible for the left panel of the triptych used a relief theme of fairly large double scrolls. This decoration is so thickly packed that the opposition between the smooth background and the relief almost escapes the eye. The leaf form is concave, the curved edges of each leaf are indicated with precision; each section has a finished, determined shape.

The central part of the triptych was executed in another manner. One notices immediately that the relief is less accentuated here than in the side panels. As a result, each part of the decoration is perceived and considered as an independent work, but the over-all homogeneity and unity of the work in no way suffers. This, in our opinion, is the essential quality of the metal casing of the Khakhuli triptych.

The light relief of the central part, the rhythm observable in the arrangement of decorative forms and their quiet pictorial nature are made more evident still by the presence of large, pierced rosettes. These rosettes, covered with a continuous, complicated pattern, fulfill an individual function, and at the same time turn one's attention to certain elements of the decoration. This decoration consists of motifs already familiar in eleventh- and twelfth-century Georgian art. The work must therefore have been made in a Georgian artistic environment with ancient, solidly rooted traditions. The Khakhuli triptych presents the essential unity of all great works of art, and forms one of the highest peaks of Georgian figurative art. It is a profoundly original, indeed, inimitable work.

KHAKHULI TRIPTYCH

THE ENAMELED FRAME

Certain fragments, sometimes assigned to another work representing a Virgin and Child, can in reality belong only to the Khakhuli triptych. The earlier hypothesis is unacceptable, for the form of the ends of the Virgin's crown and fragments of the enameled background indicate that they must have come from a *Deisis*. In any case it is certain that relief metalwork and cloisonné enamel were combined in this work, as in the Martvili *Deisis* and Encolpion-cross; the half-length figure of the Virgin was executed on a plate of repoussé gold, while the hands, face, crown, and background were in cloisonné enamel.

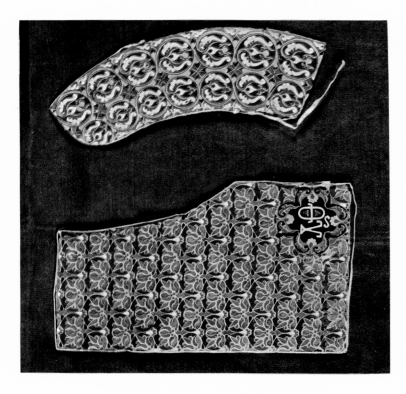

FRAGMENTS OF THE ENAMELED FRAME

The enameled fragments from an icon of the Virgin, formerly in the Botkin and Zvenigorodskoi collections, form part of the Khakhuli triptych, which was broken up and dispersed after the pillage of the monastery in 1859. Attempts have been made, using only the Zvenigorodskoi fragments, to reconstruct the icon of the Virgin. If all the fragments that have survived were assembled, it would be obvious that the Virgin was represented without the Child.

All the decorative plaques are in excellent condition. The ground motif resembles light, reddish-brown buds, enlivened by small, gracefully shaped flowers. The range of colors is severely restrained; the intensity of the dark-blue ground gives the whole a matte effect, despite the extremely translucent green smalt used for the leaves. Each element in the decoration can be viewed as a small, stylized flower, a conventionally colored, abstract decorative motif. The little crosses that link the scrolls are green, the center of each flower is red, and the edges are white. The play of colors is most harmonious and the meticulous polishing of the enameled surface gives the tones a special vibrancy.

THE VIRGIN

After its disappearance, the icon of the Virgin probably entered the Botkin collection, where it remained until 1923.

We now possess the most important fragments, in particular the face and the hands raised in prayer, and can thus reconstruct the original composition of this important work. It is the only known enamel composition of such large dimensions. One is struck by the facial type and its oval shape, by the elongated eyes and the form of the curved nose, by the arch of the exaggeratedly fine eyebrows—characteristic traits of Georgian images of the Virgin.

The enameled smalt used for the flesh, with its slight wine tone, is typically Georgian and is extremely beautiful. The enamel is very thick on the face and hands, so that small gold flanges were needed to support it. The movement of the arms and hands orients the entire composition toward the right, following the Virgin's gaze. One can thus conclude that she was portrayed in semi-profile in an attitude of prayer, with both arms raised.

THE VIRGIN. CENTRAL ICON

EMPEROR MICHAEL AND EMPRESS MARY

The lock of the case carries a small, rectangular icon ($2^{27}/_{32} \times 2^{3}/_{4}''$) representing the Byzantine Emperor Michael VII Ducas, who reigned from 1071 to 1078, and his wife, the Georgian Empress Mary, being crowned by Christ. The Saviour is seen above them, against a blue sky dotted with yellow stars. He is wearing the traditional costume, and blesses the couple with both hands. A brick-red line rims His blue halo with its white cross. Christ's name is inscribed in two small circles.

The Emperor and Empress are represented in a majestic, rigorously frontal position, wearing the ceremonial robes of the Byzantine court. The gold sash in the form of a downward-pointing shield indicates that the Empress is dressed in the costume traditionally worn by Byzantine sovereigns for their solemn appearance on the first day of the feast of Easter. Michael VII is shown in a solemn attitude, carrying the imperial standard in his right hand and a white scroll in the other. Mary has her right hand on her breast and in the other carries a scepter crowned with a four-square cross.

The shape of this cross, which stems from a very ancient tradition, constitutes one of the most characteristic elements of Georgian art. Its presence in this composition is certainly not due to chance, for in a miniature in the Paris Bibliothèque Nationale we see the Empress Mary with her second husband, holding a similar scepter in her hand. Mary carried a Georgian scepter for every ceremony in which she had to play an official part.

The Emperor Michael VII Ducas came to the throne at the age of twenty. According to his tutor, the illustrious philosopher Pessl, Michael was interested in the sciences, willingly argued with men of learning and wrote poetry and historical works. In spite of his youth he had a serious air, the appearance of a learned man, an intellectual. He is shown here as a young man with short, curly hair, a small mustache, and the hint of a beard.

His wife Mary was the daughter of the Georgian Emperor Bagrat IV. She married Michael VII Ducas, then Nikita Nicephorus Votoniat (1078–1081) when her first husband was forced to abdicate and took holy orders. The enamel icon, like the Bibliothèque Nationale miniature, renders the renowned Empress' beauty in a conventional way: the image is characterized by the tall, well-proportioned silhouette, the majestic bearing of the head, the delicate features, the expressive gaze of the black eyes, the delicate coloring of the face and its fine oval form.

✝СТЕΦω
МІХАНА
СꙔНМАРІАМ
ХЕРСІМꙊ

EMPEROR MICHAEL AND EMPRESS MARY. CENTRAL PANEL ABOVE ARCH

CHRIST ENTHRONED

The decoration of the central part of the triptych reserves the main position for a composition on the theme of the *Deisis*, which is placed below the arch of the shrine. The style and technique of these enamels relate them to the finest productions of eleventh-century Byzantine work, executed in the workshops of Constantinople in fulfillment of an imperial commission. They were certainly taken to Georgia by the Empress Mary, the daughter of the Emperor Bagrat IV, in 1072.

In the center of the triptych one can see a *Deisis* formed by three small icons: Christ Enthroned ($3^9/_{16}''$ high), flanked by the Virgin on the left and John the Baptist on the right. Christ is solemnly seated and holds a closed book, bound in yellow and decorated with precious stones, in His left hand. The folds of the garments are skillfully rendered with slender gold partitions. The facial features are conveyed with exceptional penetration. The thick black hair and the black beard with its hint at a parting lengthen the delicate outline of the oval face. The large black pupils and long, thick, sharply drawn eyebrows give the Saviour's face the stamp of greatness and severity.

The throne is sumptuously decorated with precious stones; the back is covered with white enamel bearing a decorative motif in yellow, and the feet of the throne are ornamented with precious stones of various colors. The seat is covered by a multicolored cushion, with blue at each embroidered end. The footstool is in enamel, decorated with a pattern in gold cloisonné.

CHRIST ENTHRONED. UPPER PART OF THE CENTRAL PANEL

CROSS ENAMELED WITH THE IMAGES OF CONSTANTINE AND HELENA

Below the *Deisis* there is a group of enamels that draws its unity from its subject matter and must be placed among Byzantine enamelwork of the eleventh century. In the center of this group there is a small cross enameled with the images of Constantine and Helena and surrounded by medallions of the Four Evangelists.

Constantine and Helena, in rich imperial robes, support the Holy Cross with both hands. The form of the cross, particularly the top with its three half-circles, and the base of the shaft, indicate that it was not the artist's intention to portray the discovery of the Cross on which Christ was crucified, but rather the erection by Constantine and Helena of a new cross on Golgotha.

The Emperor is a mature man. He wears a Byzantine crown of gold with jewels and pendants; his richly embroidered garments are set with precious stones which outline his figure. The Empress wears a shawl adorned with embroidery and precious stones and, on one side, the shield-shaped sash woven in gold, as was usual in ceremonial costumes. The Empress' crown has no pendants.

In the semicircular ends of the cruciform medallion there are four busts of the prophets: Isaiah at the top, Elijah to the left, Elisha on the right, and Daniel at the foot. Isaiah is an old man, Elijah is very old indeed; Elisha is mature, with black hair and beard, and wears a fur-trimmed garment, whereas Daniel is shown in fullface as a young man, with both hands raised and turned out to the viewer.

This cross is a typical example of the art of the eleventh-century Byzantine masters.

CONSTANTINE AND HELENA WITH FOUR PROPHETS. UPPER PART OF THE CENTRAL PANEL

THE VIRGIN AND SAINT THEODORE

The semicircular top of the central panel of the triptych holds two medallions of equal size (diameter $1^9/_{16}''$) representing the Virgin and Saint Theodore. They were made by the same hand, and are among the most ancient enamels in the Khakhuli triptych—in fact, they can be classed with the earliest Georgian enamels.

The Virgin is shown in half-length, both hands raised and turned out toward the viewer. The figure stands out against a background of emerald-green smalt which has the translucency of the earliest enamels. The name is written in thin gold fillets on the green ground. The face is characterized by the large eyes, thick nose, short oval shape, and long neck. The arms are rather long in relation to the rest of the body.

On either side of Mary small disks indicate the sun and moon. Above her head at left and right there are slim gold spiral motifs that certainly represent a stem with a white flower. The folds of the mantle, coarsely but clearly drawn, are definitely the work of an artist in full possession of his talents.

The medallions of the Virgin and Saint Theodore are surrounded by decorative frames composed of three concentric circles adorned with small roundels, evidently imitating pearls.

Saint Theodore is shown as a mature man, with black hair and a short, pointed beard. He has large eyes, strongly marked eyebrows and nose, and a triangular face. The nose and eyebrows are drawn with a single fillet of gold. His halo is yellow, as is Mary's. He holds a cross in his right hand, against his breast. The entire outline is rendered with one gold fillet against the ground of dark-green smalt, and on either side is a white flower and a spiral gold line representing the stem. There is a white circle beside his left shoulder.

The style of these two compositions, the way they combine the basic colors, the dark-green smalt of the background, and the manner in which the inscriptions are executed, enable us to place the medallions in the eighth century and classify them among the first manifestations of the art of cloisonné enameling in Georgia.

UPPER PART OF THE CENTRAL PANEL SHOWING THE DEISIS, CROSS WITH CONSTANTINE AND HELENA, AND MEDALLIONS OF THE FOUR EVANGELISTS

THE CRUCIFIXION

This medallion dates from the seventh or eighth century. It is in the form of a cross with arms of equal length (2 × 2″) surrounded by gold panels symmetrically arranged and adorned with small stylized flowers in cloisonné enamel. In the center, Christ, His arms outstretched, wears a long sleeveless tunic. His head is held erect and His eyes are open. To the left, below the cross, the Virgin, in dark purple, stretches out her draped arms to her Son. The halos are grayish yellow and Mary wears red shoes.

On the other side of the cross, the Apostle John extends his draped arms and bows his head slightly. At the top, two angels with reddish-brown hair, dressed in deep purple, are placed symmetrically on either side of the cross. Between them, the Hand of God, three fingers crossed in benediction, stands out against a conventionally treated dark-blue sky. Near the Hand, two circles, one white and one yellow, depict the sun and moon. Behind the Virgin and Saint John the monogram of Christ is traced in gold in two purple circles outlined in green.

In every figure the drapery is rendered in stylized folds. Anatomical proportions are not respected, and the heads are exaggeratedly large. The ovals of all faces except that of Christ are excessively shortened, so that the noses are unduly prominent. Christ's face is elongated and angular, the drawing of detail is confused and the eyes are not level with each other. The large pupils stress the fact that the Saviour is still alive. The body is in a frontal position, the head turned toward the viewer, almost in fullface.

The whole composition is treated in two main colors: dark green for the ground and deep, blackish purple for the garments. The other colors play only a complementary role and do nothing to change the monotony of the coloring. But the remarkably translucent, intense dark green of the background enlivens the whole.

CRUCIFIXION. LEFT PANEL. 7TH OR 8TH CENTURY

THE QUEEN OF HEAVEN

A comparative study of the enamels from the Khakhuli triptych leads one to set apart a particular category of Georgian work, for it is related to Byzantine work through its style and technique to such a point that it is only attached to Georgian art by a few details.

This group includes nine small enameled plaques, identical in size ($2 \times 1^9/_{16}''$), of which six show pairs of standing Apostles and the other three show the Virgin Enthroned with the Child and two Archangels. These enamels are all from the same period and definitely belong to the same series.

The Apostles and the two Archangels are arranged on either side of the main icon of the Virgin (see pages 95 and 113). The Apostles are represented in standing positions on green pedestals, their bodies held erect. Their attitude is remarkable for its plasticity, as well as the absence of frontal positions. The lower garments, the traditional mantles, freely mold the bodily outlines, and their two-toned coloring gives the figures a pictorial quality. While similar Byzantine enamels may outstrip Georgian work in fineness of execution, the latter renders drapery more pictorially and gives its figures more harmonious proportions.

These observations confirm the hypothesis that this group of enamels first saw the light in the eleventh century in some artistic milieu where the Georgian masters had fully assimilated the traditions of Byzantine cloisonné enameling, adapting them to their tastes.

When one examines this series of enamels one is struck by the way the artist has concentrated all attention on the image of the Virgin, shown as Queen of Heaven Enthroned with the Child, both ideologically and pictorially. The figures of the Apostles, though they conform to established iconographical tradition, nonetheless have individualized faces. On the other hand, the Archangels, in spite of their artistic and technical perfection, have absolutely no individuality.

Some enamel plaques on the central part of the metal covering of the triptych have survived in their original positions. Among these are the half-length figures of the Virgin and Saint Michael

LOWER PART OF THE CENTRAL PANEL. *From top, left to right:* SAINT MICHAEL, CHRIST IN JUDGMENT, THE VIRGIN, ARCHANGEL GABRIEL, THE QUEEN OF HEAVEN ENTHRONED WITH THE CHILD, ARCHANGEL MICHAEL, AND SAINT NICHOLAS

carrying crowns, and Christ in Judgment, seated on a rainbow. The figures were arranged in terms of the vertical axis of the over-all composition. Since the Virgin and Saint Michael both hold crowns in their right hands, we can conclude that they formed part of a predetermined group.

Below the figure of Christ enthroned in the clouds there is the image of the Virgin seated on a throne with the Child, but this enamel belonged to another series and was only later moved to its present position. All the enamels mentioned certainly belonged to the same composition, which could quite feasibly be reconstructed.

Under the composition of the Virgin and Child there is a bust of Saint Nicholas, wearing the traditional priestly vestments. The style and technique of execution relate this to the images of Saint Basil the Great and Saint Theodore the Theologian, but it is a little smaller ($1\frac{9}{16} \times 1\frac{3}{16}''$).

MEDALLIONS SHOWING HELLENISTIC INFLUENCES

A second group of enameled medallions, showing Hellenistic influences, consists of ten medallions arranged five by five in a half circle around the central icon of the Virgin. All these enamels belong to an ancient series, and have remained in their original positions. The semicircular arrangement fits well into the general scheme of repoussé decoration on the central part of the triptych.

In the center of the composition there is a medallion representing the Archangel Gabriel. He is the symmetrical pendant to another medallion showing the Archangel Michael. These enamels are related through their style and technique to Byzantine enamelwork, though they were made in western Georgia.

Below and to the left, the medallion of the Evangelists Luke and Mark belongs to the group described in the preceding section.

The Khakhuli triptych also incorporates several enameled medallions that do not fit into any particular composition, but nonetheless present considerable artistic interest. This category is mainly spread over the central part of the triptych and includes, notably, the figure of Gregory the Theologian. He is an old man with a long, white beard. His bare brow and severe gaze give him great expressive force.

One gold plaque attracts attention: Christ Pantocrator. It is set in a specially inserted bezel, placed asymmetrically and therefore cut off from the general composition. This icon belongs to the original decoration; it is ideologically related to the central icon of the Virgin in Prayer. The arched black eyebrows, the huge black eyes turned toward the Virgin, the straight, clearly drawn nose, abundant, black hair, and short, black, divided beard leave a pleasant over-all impression. The style and technique of this medallion of Christ Pantocrator enable one to place it in the first half of the twelfth century.

UPPER RIGHT-HAND SIDE OF THE CENTRAL PANEL. *From top left to bottom left:* ARCHANGEL,
CHRIST PANTOCRATOR, ARCHANGEL GABRIEL, GREGORY THE THEOLOGIAN, AND THE
EVANGELISTS JOHN AND MARK

CHRIST AND SAINTS MARK (*above*), PETER (*left*), PAUL (*right*), AND LUKE (*below*).
ENCOLPION-CROSS ON THE LEFT PANEL. 10TH CENTURY

There can be no doubt that the encolpion-cross, split in two and placed on the two side-panels of the triptych, must be considered a Georgian enamel. Both fragments are the same size ($5^{1}/_{8} \times 3^{9}/_{16}$"). One of these crosses shows a Crucifixion; Christ is in the center, His eyes closed and His body barely hung on the cross, the left foot slightly forward and the arms sagging. The upper part of the figure is damaged, especially the left shoulder. The halo is light blue outlined with red; the black hair and round beard frame a fine-featured face. The thighs are covered with a light-blue loin cloth. The cross itself is dark, with the traditional Golgotha and Adam's skull at the foot.

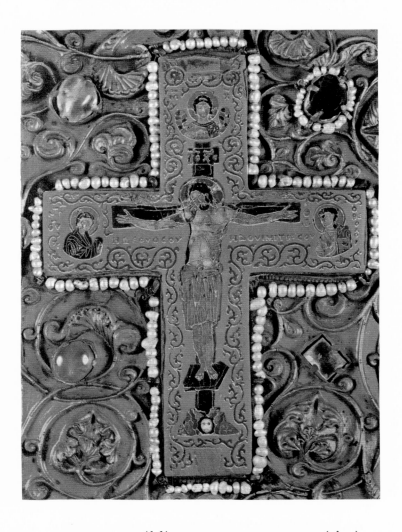

CRUCIFIXION WITH THE VIRGIN (*left*), ARCHANGEL GABRIEL (*above*), AND JOHN THE
EVANGELIST. ENCOLPION-CROSS ON THE RIGHT PANEL. 10TH CENTURY

Above, the Archangel Gabriel is shown fullface with an orb in his right hand. To the left, the
weeping Virgin, seen in profile, reaches out her veiled hands to her Son. On the other branch of
the cross there is a bust of John the Evangelist, who carries a closed book in his left hand.

On the other cross, Christ is surrounded by Saint Mark above, Saint Peter to the left, Saint Paul
to the right, and Saint Luke below.

Lord, glorify the Emperor Kvirik, reads the inscription in Georgian, and *Christ, aid Thy slave,
magister Kvirik,* in Greek. The study of these inscriptions and other historical sources permits us
to date this cross in the tenth century, and assign it to a Georgian enameler.

FOUR APOSTLES

On the lower frame of the central panel of the triptych, two plaques have survived, each bearing two Apostles. They formed part of a homogeneous series originally placed in the center of the frame, but dispersed at an early stage in the triptych's history.

The two plaques show, respectively, Peter and John the Theologian, Paul and Matthew. They are the same size ($3^1/_8 \times 2^3/_{16}''$) and their upper edges are similarly rounded. The four figures are

shown in a standing position, turned toward the center of the composition. These plaques must have figured elsewhere before being used in the decoration of the Khakhuli triptych. Peter holds a scroll in his left hand and gives a blessing, crossing three fingers of his right hand. On his tunic one can see a narrow band adorned with precious stones; let us remember that this is the characteristic sign of the Apostle Peter. Beside Saint Peter, John the Theologian is shown as a very old man.

The Apostles Paul and Matthew are seen standing in the same attitude as the other two. The style and technique of these two plaques relates them to Byzantine art of the eleventh century.

SAINT PETER

In this medallion the Apostle Peter is represented in accordance with the traditional type: gray hair and eyebrows, short, slightly wavy beard, all rendered in a blue-gray smalt. His green halo is set in an irregular brick-red outline. He wears a green tunic with a yellow band, and a deep-blue mantle.

Peter crosses three fingers of his right hand before his breast to give a benediction, and holds a white scroll in his left hand. He is in a slightly oblique position, his body barely turned.

The enlarged black pupils give a severe expression to his face.

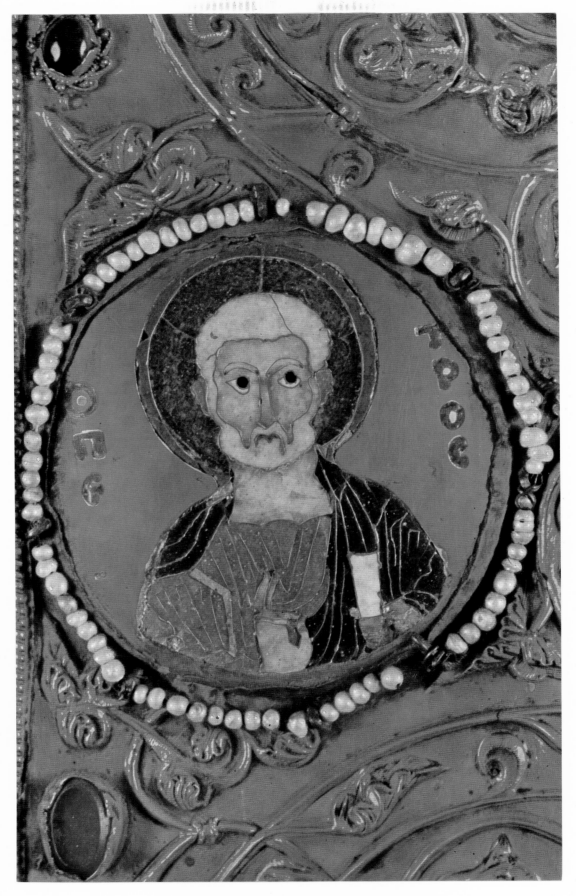

MEDALLION OF SAINT PETER. UPPER PART OF THE LEFT PANEL

THE DECORATION OF THE TRIPTYCH

Decoration has a particularly important part to play in the artistic conception of the triptych. The ornamental nature of the panels is stressed by the original repoussé work, the symmetrical arrangement of large decorative crosses, and medallions in specially placed settings around the edges. The arrangement of the medallions, ten to each surface, was established by the artist before starting to work.

Out of the twenty medallions, only seventeen are ancient; the other three are Russian painted enamels from the second half of the nineteenth century. Since they are all the same size (diameter $2^{15}/_{32}$″) and resemble each other in technique and coloring, they can be considered as one group. It is also to be noted that several characters are represented more than once (Christ three times, John the Theologian, Matthew, and Simon twice each) which seems to indicate that this was an over-all composition.

Three medallions—Christ, the Virgin, and John the Baptist—form a homogeneous composition on the theme of the *Deisis*. Although these plaques have not been grouped together, we can suppose that originally they occupied the lower part of the panel. Such an arrangement of the three figures would have constituted an extremely rare version of the *Deisis*, for the Virgin would have been to Christ's *left*, with John the Baptist to His right.

Furthermore, the figures of the Apostles can be divided into two groups—depending on whether they are shown fullface or in profile—treated in different styles and colors. Even though the style and iconographical character of these enamels suggest the existence of two distinct groups, they can all be placed in the same period. They were executed about 1150 in western Georgia by Georgian artists, and were related to other enamels from west Georgian workshops—those on the icons of Gelati and Tsalendgika, and the Saint Michael icon from Jumati.

The decorative enamels, which vary in size, are distributed over the surface of the triptych in strict symmetry, and the relationships thus established between them are rigorously maintained. All the crosses have come down to us in their original positions. The artist responsible for the covering of the triptych must have taken them into account; their size corresponds to the decorative design proposed by the master repoussé workers in terms of the free spaces available.

The large crosses are on the side panels, particularly where the relief is most emphatic and broadly drawn. On the central part, where the decoration presents a much smaller pattern and less relief, the lower corners hold two small crosses and, in the angles below the arch, four enamel plaques, in the center of which enamel lozenges are set. The lower frame of the central part incorporates two small crosses consisting of four triangular enameled plates. They are symmetrically arranged, and each has a large stone in the center. In the same part, below the image of Saint Basil (a late-nineteenth-century Russian work), an enameled lozenge carries a motif identical in design and coloring to the crosses just mentioned. Two small filigree panels, dating from the twelfth century and decorated with precious stones, also figure in this passage of the decoration.

The four square plaques fixed in the corners of the hollowed-out area for the icon, have all

ENAMELED CROSS ON THE RIGHT PANEL

survived, except the one that was at the top left. They are identical and certainly formed part of the original decoration. Toward the top of the right panel, there is a gold plate with a gold filigree cross adorned with stones in its center (Russian work of the mid-twelfth century). This entire plaque belongs to the original decoration; it is placed level with the Crucifixion on the left panel. Lastly, the decoration of the triptych seems to arrive at a conclusion with the small panel, worked in filigree and adorned with jewels, placed to the left of the foot of the arch in the central part and, on the right panel, with two gold plaques adorned with colored stones.

The primary role, however, is played by the large, symmetrically placed crosses. The large cross on the left panel ($9^7/_8 \times 7^7/_8''$) is ornamented in the center and at the extremities with circular gold medallions surrounded by squares of dark-green smalt. In the center of each medallion there is a plaque in shallow relief, whose design is repeated without modification. The plaque from the central medallion is badly damaged, and those that adorn the right and lower branches of the cross have been replaced with stones.

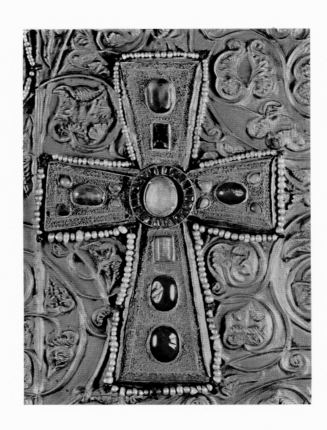

FILIGREE CROSS ON THE LEFT PANEL

The gold cross adorned with delicate filigree that can be seen a little below the large, decorative cross ($5^7/_8 \times 3^{15}/_{16}$") is set with precious stones and belongs to the original decoration of the triptych. On the left panel, another cross in gold filigree is almost identical in shape and proportions ($9^5/_8 \times 7^9/_{32}$") to the large one on the right panel. Filigree serves purely as a background on this cross, over which the precious stones are arranged in rigorous order. The outline is picked out with a double row of large and small pearls, also systematically arranged. The central medallion and the four on the extremities incorporate plaques of colored stones arranged around one large, uncut gem. The branches of the cross are decorated with precious stones, particularly large, semi-cylindrical emeralds disposed in pairs.

A little below this cross there is another, square this time, whose surface is almost entirely covered with an enameled pattern ($5^1/_2 \times 5^1/_2$"). The arms were worked separately, then skillfully joined by a medallion in which a large stone is set.

Another cross ($6^{11}/_{16} \times 4^{17}/_{32}$") fills the left corner of the central part of the triptych, and has a medallion with the bust of Christ (diameter 1") at the center. To the right of the central part, another enameled cross ($5^3/_8 \times 3^3/_8$") bears in its center a square plaque with the image of the Apostle Paul ($3/_4 \times 3/_4$").

THE KHAKHULI TRIPTYCH is a major work of Georgian medieval art. It is also a work of universal value, for its significance is not limited to the context of ancient Georgian culture.

The decoration consists of various motifs that are frequently found in Georgian repoussé work of the eleventh and twelfth centuries. However, neither historical nor artistic analyses of this ornamental system have led to the discovery of imitations, direct or indirect, such as usually follow in the wake of genuine masterpieces. The repoussé work on the Khakhuli triptych is outstanding for its originality and the unity of its over-all composition. In this it is inimitable, like the ornamentation on the frame of the icon of the Saviour from Antshiskhati, the work of the renowned Beka Opizari.

We must repeat that ornamentation accords an important place to decorative and figurative enamels, as well as cut and precious stones: The arrangement of these elements over the surface of the covering was based on principles of rigorous symmetry, taking into account the dimensions, shape, and even coloring of the enameled ornaments. Attentive examination shows that most of the ornaments are set in the positions chosen by the artists when they drew up the general plan of the triptych. They had at their disposal enamels of different periods, origins, and styles. In addition to this, they could call on a whole series of Georgian enamels (the group of twenty arranged around the edges of the panels). Byzantine enamels were placed mainly in the central section, around the part hollowed out to hold the icon; they date mostly from the eleventh century, but some can be assigned to the twelfth.

The eleventh-century Byzantine enamels are outstandingly important by virtue of the quality of their execution—in particular, the icon of Michael VII Ducas and the Empress Mary, the *Deisis* composition, and the cross with Constantine and Helena, all of which occupy the central part of the triptych.

On the whole, however, the Georgian enamels constitute the decorative basis of the triptych. While some date from the seventh, eighth, and ninth centuries, most of them were made between the tenth and twelfth. They can be classed in different groups, according to style and manner, so that one is able to follow the evolution of Georgian enamelwork through the most important periods of its history.

BIBLIOGRAPHY

Note: Titles preceded by an asterisk (*) have been translated from the Russian

*AMIRANASHVILI, Shalva. *Beka Opizari*, Tiflis, 1956

*———. *Georgian Cloisonné Enamels*, 25th International Congress of Orientalists, Moscow, 1960

*———. *History of Georgian Art*, Moscow, 1950

*———. *History of Monumental Painting in Georgia*, Tiflis, 1937

*APAKIDZE, A.; GOBEJISHVILI, G.; KALANDADZE, A.; AND LOMTATIDZE, G. *Archaeological Monuments Discovered in Excavations in Mtskhet'i Between 1937 and 1946* (Summary of archaeological research), Tiflis

*BELIAEV, D. "Ceremonial Appearances of Byzantine Emperors in the Church of Saint Sophia in the Ninth and Tenth Centuries," *Bulletin of the Russian Society of Archaeologists*, VI (1893), St. Petersburg

*BERDZENISHVILI, N. "An Eleventh-Century Document from Mtskhet'i," *Bulletin of the Georgian National Museum*, VI (1931), Tiflis

BLANCHOT, I. *Les Bijoux anciens*, Paris, 1929

Botkin Collection, St. Petersburg, 1911

BROSSET, M. *Voyage Archéologique* (report)

CECCELLI, C. *La Cattedra di Massimiano*, Rome, 1936

CELLINI, BENVENUTO. *I trattati dell'oreficeria e della scultura*, Florence, 1893

*CHUBINASHVILI, G. *Georgian Repoussé Work of the Thirteenth and Fourteenth Centuries*, Tiflis, 1957–59

———. "Ein Goldschmiedtriptychon des VIII.–IX. Jahrhunderts aus Martvili," *Zeitschrift für bildende Kunst*, Leipzig, 1930

COMNENIA, ANNA. *The Alexiad*, trans. E. A. S. Davies, London, 1928

DALTON, O. M. *Byzantine Art and Archaeology*, Oxford, 1911

———. *East Christian Art*, Oxford, 1923

———. *Un réliquaire en or émaillé* (studies in memory of N. Kondakov), Seminarium Kondakovianum, Prague, 1926

Das Münster, 1955

DIEHL, C. *Manuel d'art byzantin*, Vol. II, Paris, 1926

Early Christian and Byzantine Art. (An exhibition held at the Baltimore Museum of Art), Baltimore, 1947

*ELCHIN, DEACON. Report in *Russian Ambassadorial Missions in the 16th and 17th Centuries*, Moscow-Leningrad, 1954

*GORDEEV, D. *On Classifying the Enamels from the Khakhuli Triptych*, School of Oriental Studies, Kharkov, 1928

———. "Description de cinq médaillons émaillés avec inscriptions géorgiennes se trouvant sur l'icône du Sauveur, conservée au sanctuaire du monastère de Ghélati," *Orient chrétien*, Vol. V, 1917

GRABAR, A. *L'Empereur dans l'art byzantin*, Paris, 1936

*JAVAKISHVILI, I. *History of the Georgian People*, Tiflis, 1948

*JOBADZE-TSITSISHVILI, V. "The Enamels of the Museo Lázaro Goldiano," *Soviet Art*, No. 4, Tiflis, 1948

*JORDANIA, F. *Chronicle and Other Documents Relating to Georgia*, Tiflis, 1892

*KARTLIS OF CHOVREB. *Index of the Empress Mary*, ed. E. Takaishvili, Tiflis, 1906

*———. *The "Matiane Kartlisai" Georgian Manuscript*, ed. T. Kaukhchivili, Tiflis, 1955

*KAUKHCHIVILI, T. *Greek Inscriptions in Georgia*, 1951

*KENIA, R. "The Repoussé Work on the Khakhuli Icon," *Studies of the Georgian Academy of Sciences*, Vol. XXII, 1959

125

*KIRPICHNIKOV, A. *Literary Parallels with the Deisis in East and West*, 1893

*KONDAKOV, N. P. *An Archaeological Expedition in Syria and Palestine*, St. Petersburg

*———. *History and Monuments of Byzantine Enamelwork* (Byzantine Enamels in the Zvenigorodskoi Collection), 1887–92

*———. *Iconography of the Mother of God*, St. Petersburg, 1915–16

*——— AND BAKRADZE, D. *Inventory of Ancient Monuments in Georgian Churches and Monasteries*, St. Petersburg, 1890

*——— AND TOLSTOY, I. *Russian Antiquities in Artistic Monuments: Christian Antiquities in the Crimea, Caucasus, and Kiev*, St. Petersburg, 1891

*KUFTIN, B. *The Excavations at T'rialet'i: I. Tentative Chronological Classification of Finds*, Tiflis

List of Treasures from Georgian Museums (Treasures sent to Paris in 1921 by the Menshevik Government and restored to Georgia in 1945), Tiflis, 1946

MACULEVITCH, L. "Monuments perdus de Dżumati," *Byzantion*, II, 1926

*MAKARENKO, N. "Exhibition of Ancient Ecclesiastical Objects in the Baron Shtiglitza Museum," *Olden Times*, 1915

MOREY, C. *Early Christian Art*, London, 1942

MUÑOZ, A. *L'Arte bizantina nella mostra di Grottaferrata*, Rome, 1906

OMONT, N. *Evangiles avec peintures byzantines du XIe siècle*

*POLIEVKTOV, M. *The Diplomatic Mission of Squire Toloshanov and Deacon Ievlev in Imeret'i, 1650–52*, Tiflis, 1926

PORPHYROGENITUS, CONSTANTINE. *De caeremoniis aulae byzantinae*

ROSENBERG, M. *Geschichte der Goldschmiedekunst auf technischer Grundlage*, Abteilung, Zellenschmelz I–II, Frankfort, 1921

*RYBAKOV, V. *Crafts in Ancient Russia*, Soviet Academy of Sciences, Moscow, 1948

*SCHMIDT, F. "The Deisis in Russian and Byzantine Art," *Bulletin of the University of Kharkov*, 1914

SCHULZ, J. *Der byzantinische Zellenschmelz*, Frankfort, 1890

*SKABALANOVITCH, N. *The Byzantine Empire and the Church*, St. Petersburg, 1834

*SMIRNOV, I. *The Akhalgori Treasure*, Tiflis, 1934

*TAKAISHVILI, E. "An Archaeological Expedition in Mingrelia," *Ancient Georgia*, 1912–14

*———. "The Enameled Image of the Emperor George of Imeret'i," *Bulletin of the Caucasian Section of the Russian Society of Archaeologists*, 1904

TARSHNISHVILI, M. *Typicon, Grégoire Pacouriani*, Louvain, 1954

THEOPHILUS (Priest). *Schedula diversarum artium*, Vienna, 1874

*TOLSTOY, I., AND KONDAKOV, N. P. *Russian Antiquities in Artistic Monuments: Christian Antiquities in the Crimea, Caucasus, and Kiev*, St. Petersburg, 1891

*TSAGARELI, A. *Monuments Concerning Ancient Georgia in Syria, the Holy Land, and Sinai*, St. Petersburg, 1904

*TSERETELI, G. "Complete Collection of Inscriptions on the Walls and Stones of the Monastery of Gelati, Together with the Texts of Manuscripts from the Same Monastery," *Oriental Antiquities*, Vol. I, Moscow, 1891

VAN DER MEER, F. *Majestas Domini*, Paris, 1938